Gratitude

♥   ♥   ♥

BOOKS, AUDIOS, AND VIDEOS
BY LOUISE L. HAY

❤ Books ❤

The Aids Book: Creating a Positive Approach
Colors & Numbers
A Garden of Thoughts: My Affirmation Journal
Gratitude: A Way of Life (Louise L. Hay and Friends)
Heal Your Body
Heart Thoughts: A Treasury of Inner Wisdom
Life! Reflections on Your Journey
Love Your Body
Love Yourself, Heal Your Life Workbook
Loving Thoughts for Health and Healing
Loving Thoughts for Increasing Prosperity
Loving Thoughts for Loving Yourself
Loving Thoughts for a Perfect Day
Meditations to Heal Your Life
101 Power Thoughts
The Power Is Within You
You Can Heal Your Life

❤ Coloring Books/Audiocassettes for Children ❤

Lulu and the Ant: A Message of Love
Lulu and the Dark: Conquering Fears
Lulu and Willy the Duck: Learning Mirror Work

❤ Audiocassettes ❤

Aids: A Positive Approach
Cancer: Discovering Your Healing Power
Elders of Excellence
Empowering Women
Feeling Fine Affirmations
Gift of the Present *with Joshua Leeds*
Heal Your Body (Audio Book)
Life! Reflections on Your Journey
Love Your Body (Audio Book)
Loving Yourself
Meditations for Personal Healing
Meditations to Heal Your Life (Audio Book)

Morning and Evening Meditations
Overcoming Fears
The Power Is Within You (Audio Book)
Self Healing
Songs of Affirmation *with Joshua Leeds*
What I Believe/Deep Relaxation
You Can Heal Your Life (Audio Book)
You Can Heal Your Life Study Course

❤ Conversations on Living Lecture Series ❤
Change and Transition
Dissolving Barriers
The Forgotten Child Within
How to Love Yourself
The Power of Your Spoken Word
Receiving Prosperity
Totality of Possibilities
Your Thoughts Create Your Life

❤ Personal Power Through Imagery Series ❤
Anger Releasing
Forgiveness/Loving the Inner Child

❤ Subliminal Mastery Series ❤
Feeling Fine Affirmations
Love Your Body Affirmations
Safe Driving Affirmations
Self-Esteem Affirmations
Self-Healing Affirmations
Stress-Free Affirmations

❤ Videocassettes ❤
Dissolving Barriers
Doors Opening: A Positive Approach to Aids
Receiving Prosperity
You Can Heal Your Life Study Course
Your Thoughts Create Your Life

Available at your local bookstore, or call:
(800) 654-5126

Gratitude

A Way of Life

by

LOUISE L. HAY and Friends

Compiled and Edited by Jill Kramer

Hay House, Inc.
Carlsbad, CA

Published and distributed in the United States by:

Hay House, Inc., P.O. Box 5100, Carlsbad, CA 92018-5100
(800) 654-5126

Edited by: Jill Kramer   Designed by: Jenny Richards

Library of Congress Cataloging-in-Publication Data

Hay, Louise L.
       Gratitude : a way of life / by Louise L. Hay and friends.
          p.   cm.
    ISBN   1-56170-309-5
    1. Gratitude.   I.   Title.
    BJ1533.G8H38   1996
    179'.9—dc20   96-22530
                                            CIP

ISBN 1-56170-309-5

99 98 97 96   4 3 2 1
First Printing, October 1996

❤ CONTENTS ❤

❤ INTRODUCTION ❤

by Louise L. Hay

I am so pleased to be sharing this very special book with my friends...and the world. All of the profits from this book will benefit my non-profit organization, The Hay Foundation, which diligently works to improve the quality of life for many people, including those with aids, and battered women.

As you read through the lovely, inspirational thoughts in this book, I hope that you will take the time to think about all the things that you have to be grateful for in *your* life.

I know that I always make a point of spending part of each day...

...*Thanking the Universe*

Louise L. Hay *is a metaphysical lecturer and teacher and the bestselling author of 17 books, including YOU CAN HEAL YOUR LIFE and LIFE! REFLECTIONS ON YOUR JOURNEY. Since beginning her career as a Science of Mind minister in 1981, she has assisted thousands of people in discovering and using the full potential of their own creative powers for personal growth and self-healing. Louise's works have been translated into 25 different languages in 33 countries throughout the world. She is the owner and founder of Hay House, Inc., a publishing company devoted to disseminating books, audios, videos, and other materials that help heal the planet.*

I have noticed that the Universe loves gratitude. The more grateful you are, the more goodies you get. When I say "goodies," I don't mean only material things. I mean all the people, places, and experiences that make life so wonderfully worth living. You know how great you feel when your life is filled with love and joy and health and creativity, and you get the green lights and the parking places. This is how our lives are meant to be lived. The Universe is a generous, abundant giver, and it likes to be appreciated.

Think about how you feel when you give a friend a present. If the person looks at it and her face falls, or she says, "Oh, it's not my size, or not my color, or I never use anything like that, or is that all there is," then I am sure you will have little desire to ever give her a present again. However, if her eyes dance with delight, and she is pleased and thankful, then every time you see something she would like, you want to give it to her, whether you actually do so or not.

Gratitude brings more to be grateful about. It increases your abundant life. Lack of gratitude, or complaining, brings little to rejoice about. Complainers always find that they have little good in their life, or they do not enjoy what they *do* have. The Universe always gives us what we believe we deserve. Many of us have been raised to look at what we do not have and to feel only lack. We come from a belief in scarcity and then wonder why our lives are so empty. If we believe that "I don't have, and I won't be happy until I do...," then we are putting our lives on hold. What the Universe hears is: "I don't have, and I am not happy," and that is what you get more of.

For quite some time now, I've been accepting every compliment and every present with: "I accept with joy and pleasure and gratitude." I have learned that the Universe loves this expression, and I constantly get the most wonderful presents.

When I awaken in the morning, the first thing I do before I even open my eyes is to thank my bed for a good night's sleep. I am grateful for the warmth and comfort it has given me. From that beginning, it is easy to think of many, many more things that I am grateful for. By the time I have gotten out of bed, I have probably expressed gratitude for 80 or 100 different people, places, things, and experiences in my life. This is a great way to start the day.

In the evening, just before sleep, I go through the day, blessing and being grateful for each experience. I also forgive myself if I feel that I made a mistake or said something inappropriate or made a decision that was not the best. This exercise fills me with "warm fuzzies," and I drift off to sleep like a happy baby.

We even want to be grateful for the lessons we have. Don't run from lessons; they are little packages of treasure that have been given to us. As we learn from them, our lives change for the better. I now rejoice whenever I see another portion of the dark side of myself. I know that it means that I am ready to let go of something that has been hindering my life. I say, "Thank you for showing me this, so I can heal it and move on." So, whether the lesson is a "problem" that has cropped up, or an opportunity to see an old, negative pattern within us that it is time to let go of, rejoice!

Let's spend as many moments as we can every day being grateful for all the good that is in our lives. If you have little in your life now, it will increase. If you have an abundant life now, *it* will increase. This is a win-win situation. You are happy, and the Universe is happy. Gratitude increases your abundance.

Start a gratitude journal. Write something to be grateful about each day. On a daily basis, tell someone how grateful you are for something. Tell sales clerks, waiters, postal workers, employers and employees, friends, family, and perfect strangers. Share the gratitude secret. Let's help make this a world of grateful, thankful giving and receiving...for everyone!

The Healing Power of Helping Others

Harold Bloomfield, M.D.

Harold Bloomfield, M.D., is one of the leading psychospiritual educators of our time. A Yale-trained psychiatrist, Harold is an adjunct professor of psychology at Union Graduate School. From his first book, TM, which was an international bestseller, to his book HOW TO SURVIVE THE LOSS OF A LOVE, Harold has proven to be at the forefront of many valuable, spiritual self-help movements worldwide. His books, MAKING PEACE WITH YOUR PARENTS, MAKING PEACE WITH YOURSELF, and MAKING PEACE IN YOUR STEP-FAMILY, introduced personal and family peace-

making to millions. His latest books include HOW TO HEAL DEPRESSION and THE POWER OF 5, the latter being the source for his contribution to GRATITUDE. THE POWER OF 5 is co-authored by Robert K. Cooper, Ph.D., and is published by Rodale Press.

A regular weekly habit of helping others may be as important to your health and longevity as regular exercise and good nutrition—and helping others offers value to the health of your community and the world as well. In fact, it may be a key to ending the deadly cycle of fear, isolationism, and violence that is rampant in our individualistic society. Lending a helping hand to other people is good for your own vitality, heart, and immune system. People who do regular volunteer work show a dramatic increase in life expectancy over those who perform no such services for others.

Focusing on others can help get you out of the common state of gridlock from self-centeredness on family, career, and financial worries or stresses. Helping others tends to improve mood, deepen optimism, and nourish us with a sense of genuine gratitude. Helping someone less capable can enhance your appreciation of your own skills, knowledge, competence, and strengths. The primary benefits of helping seem to be in the *process* rather than the *outcome.* By that I mean the payoffs—for the one being helped and for you—arise primarily from the moment-to-moment interactions in helping rather than on whether a social condition is "fixed" or not.

Contrary to popular opinion, helping others does not require a huge commitment of time. All you need is a personal plan that can range from doing scheduled work with a volunteer organization to spontaneous acts of generosity and kindness throughout the week. In choosing a type of helping activity that will heighten good feelings and tend to keep you helping every week, create personal contact with the people you help. To keep your enthusiasm high, make the helping activity something that appeals to your own interests or skills.

Another wonderful thing you can do is to arrange for five minutes in private to tell a loved one many of the specific reasons you appreciate him or her. What meaning and inspiration can you and your spouse find in the detailed history of your relationship? Make a list ahead of time so you can "bathe" your loved one in appreciation. Some suggestions:

❤ *What attracted you to your lover in the first place?*

❤ *What specific qualities about him or her do you admire the most?*

❤ *What were some of the highlights—and moments of laughter and fun—when you first began dating?*

💜 *What made the relationship worth pursuing?*

💜 *How did your partner help the two of you overcome any differences or obstacles along the way?*

💜 *What are your favorite memories of your first year in the relationship?*

💜 *What efforts by your partner have helped the relationship make it through the difficult times?*

Once you've made a list of specific experiences and qualities that you appreciate in your loved one, share the results. One rule: The partner who is listening must not make judgments or negate any of the appreciative comments ("I'm not *really* that considerate..." "I never looked *that* sexy; besides now I've got to lose ten pounds..."). Then find another time to trade roles, and give your spouse five minutes to express some of the specific things she or he appreciates about you. This simple exercise helps you stop taking each other for granted and can effectively reawaken an awareness of the qualities in your partner—and yourself—that form the shared, sometimes hidden, foundation of your love.

Thank God for What Doesn't Need Healing

Joan Borysenko, Ph.D.

Joan Borysenko, Ph.D., is the president of Mind/Body Health Sciences, Inc., and the author of five bestselling books, including THE POWER OF THE MIND TO HEAL; FIRE IN THE SOUL; and MINDING THE BODY, MENDING THE MIND. She co-founded and is a former director of the Mind/Body Clinic at New England Deaconess Hospital and was an instructor in medicine at Harvard Medical School. Joan is a cancer cell biologist, a licensed psychologist, and a yoga/ meditation instructor.

❤ ❤ ❤

One clear winter's day, I decided to take a walk in the tiny Colorado wilderness town where I live. The sky was a shade of azure blue peculiar to the higher elevations of the Rockies. The early March sun poured like liquid gold through the limbs of tall spruce, creating dancing patterns of light in the delicate crystals of freshly fallen snow. Mountain peaks rose majestically in sculpted layers of greens and grays, piercing clouds that hung like fairy mist in the enchanted valleys below.

Marching resolutely down the road, I was all but blind to the extraordinary beauty. Attempting to relax before driving down the mountain to undergo a breast biopsy at the local hospital, I was actually reviewing the endless menu of dire medical possibilities that might materialize. As my mind slid into well-worn patterns of awfulizing, it gathered momentum. Not only might my body be in mortal danger, but my life wasn't working so well in other ways either. Not only did the glass seem half empty, but the remaining water appeared downright polluted!

My youngest son, although nearly 22, was terribly upset by the recent separation of my husband of nearly 24 years and myself. My fault, of course. I felt overworked and burned out. Also my fault. What kind of crazy life had I managed to create—especially when I am supposed to be some kind of role model for others? Guilt, fear, anger, and disappointment joined the cacophony of inner voices accompanying me down the road on my attempt at a mindful relaxation walk.

I was rudely awakened from my toxic reverie by a searing pain in my hindquarters. Perfectly focused on my well-rehearsed mental movies, I had been completely unaware of the speedy approach of a large German shepherd who bounded up and bit me unceremoniously on the behind. My mental movie department immediately began to run a feature film starring my bare buttocks being sutured in the Boulder Community Hospital emergency room, while I was simultaneously being injected with huge doses of tetanus toxoid and rabies vaccine. I would, no doubt, miss my biopsy and have to undergo that second round of medical torture on another day.

I reached down into my pants expecting to encounter a sticky mass of blood. Strangely, my hand emerged perfectly clean. Energized by sudden hope, I slipped behind a bush and pulled my pants down. While a large red welt, framed by the impression of a perfect set of canine teeth, graced my derrière, the skin was magically unbroken. With a yelp of pure joy, I pulled up my pants and burst from the bushes with a whoop of uncensored gratitude. No emergency room. No tetanus shots. No slow death from rabies. I could get to the biopsy on time. Lucky me.

Suddenly, the entire scene seemed hilariously funny. The dog was transformed from a nasty cur to a Divine Messenger. "Wake up, you silly human! Feel the sun on your face and the wind in your hair. You are alive, and the world is beautiful. The mountains are alive, and the day is young. There are endless possibilities to experience and worlds to create."

The veil of forgetfulness dropped from my eyes, and I suddenly found myself overwhelmed with gratitude for the gift of life. Every breath was precious. Every step was a miracle. The stresses I had obsessed about seemed like cleverly constructed challenges that beckoned me to create life more mindfully and authentically. Peace settled around me like a down quilt, and I felt held by unseen arms.

Gratitude is indeed like a gearshift that can move our mental mechanism from obsession to peacefulness, from stuckness to creativity, from fear to love. The ability to relax and be mindfully present in the moment comes naturally when we are grateful. One of the most delightful aspects of my Jewish heritage is the saying of Brachot, blessings or prayers of thanksgiving throughout the day. These are praises of God for creating a world of infinite wonder and possibility. There is a blessing upon seeing a star or a rainbow. There is a blessing for the gifts of food, wine, and water. There is even a blessing upon going to the bathroom for internal organs that function so well! I like to add impromptu blessings throughout the day. Thanks to the Infinite Creative Universe, the Unknown Mystery we call God, for creating German shepherds to wake us up at the most unlikely times!

I once attended a Charismatic Catholic healing service during which the priest led us in a prayer of gratitude for all the things in our life that did not need healing. Thank God the German shepherd didn't break the skin. Thank God the breast biopsy was negative. Thank God I am healthy and able to remember—at least from time to time—that gratitude is the key to peace, joy, and creative choice. May you also be blessed with the gift of remembering. Take a moment tonight, before you go to bed, and give thanks for five things in your life that don't need healing. Throughout the day, when you find yourself stuck in awfulizing about the things that seem wrong, remember to say a prayer of gratitude for all the things that are right.

Grateful Reflections

Carolyn A. Bratton

Carolyn A. Bratton is the co-founder of Lifestream Center—Roanoke, Virginia's only holistic healing center; and she is an ordained minister as well. A graduate of two of Louise Hay's Intensive Training Programs, for several years Carolyn has been conducting workshops and seminars in both the United States and abroad based on Louise Hay's book YOU CAN HEAL YOUR LIFE and James Redfield's bestseller THE CELESTINE PROPHECY.

When I look back on my life and see how incredibly it has unfolded, with all of the lessons I have been taught by the Masters who have helped me look at the dark corners of my life, I am in awe at this wonderful thing called Life! So, yes, I am indeed grateful, at some times more than others, but nevertheless, I am filled with humbling gratitude that I have the opportunity to be acting out my life at this most auspicious time in the history of our planet.

Gratitude is something that is so important to one's quality of life. For me, I know that when I am in gratitude, my channel is wide open for any and all good that could make its way to me. The opposite is also true. If nothing is happening in my life, all I have to do is check the gratitude barometer, and there it is. A closed heart renders a closed lifeline to the Source of all happiness, joy, and bliss.

It has become my practice to operate in the "act as if" mode—that is, I act as if I am grateful even when I am finding it difficult to muster up the fuzzy feeling that just naturally comes when one is thankful and grateful. And before too long, I AM grateful!

I have found that it is an interesting ritual to sing a tune to all the things I am grateful for when I am riding in my car. I begin my song with a simple thank you for whatever, and that whatever seems to unclog an endless supply of things that I am grateful for. This practice is especially uplifting if I am not in a particularly grateful mood. The tune or ditty becomes quite creative, and soon I find that I am smiling at myself, which, by the way, is a great way to nurture and amuse your own best friend—YOU!

Another thing I love to do is to say thank you! And I would add to that the word *yes!* As Louise Hay says in her wonderful affirmation, "I say YES to Life, and Life says YES to me!" With that kind of chemistry floating around in your head, your body, the ethers—emanating from you and touching everyone and everything—it's bound to come back to you, and come back multiplied!

We sometimes forget that we are God-beings, and that the intent of the Creator was for us to enjoy this thing called Life! Our lessons can be filled with joy instead of so much pain, and when our attitude comes from a loving, grateful, and appreciative place of the heart, the Masters and the Angels and the Guides can assist us even more. When we ask for their assistance, we can be ever so grateful for this Planetary Hierarchy that is more than willing to help us. It is then that we realize that we are never alone on our path.

I find that the more willing I am to be grateful for the small things in my life, the bigger stuff just seems to show up from unexpected sources, and I am constantly looking forward to each day with all of the surprises that keep coming my way!

So, if your life is not working for you right now, it could be because that gratitude attitude needs a loving adjustment. Decree and affirm that you are willing to be more grateful, and watch Life's gifts come to you. Also, be more willing to be giving. The more grateful you are, the more good will come to you; the more you give, the more you receive.

Life—how good it is! And so it is. And so be it!

Patty

Lee Carroll

Lee Carroll is the author of the KRYON book series, a love-filled suite of works that speak of the good news for planet Earth. Found in metaphysical stores all over the planet, the books have become a source for renewed hope as we move into the uncertainty of the next millennium. His latest work is THE PARABLES OF KRYON.

There was no hope, I was told. It was only a matter of time before the hand of God reached out to take the small remaining spark of life from my deteriorating body. Each day I lay in the same spot staring at the wall next to me...waiting for Patty. She arrived at about 3:00 P.M. each day to read to me, hold my hand, wipe my brow, and speak kind words of reassurance. She left at 6:00 P.M. Each night I had to pretend it was okay for her to go, and then try to figure out why I was being served dinner yet again—a seeming waste of food.

Patty knew I was dying, and yet her eyes sparkled with hope, and her words were always cheerful. Even in the midst of my most painful times, she smiled and winked that special wink that said, "Stop all this self-pity stuff, and come up to my level to meet me." Oddly enough, I did—each time. It wasn't hard to do when I had a vibrant human being in front of me who cared about my last days...like it mattered. I dreaded the visiting relatives—the awkward silence, the downcast eyes, and the sorrow they broadcast every time they visited. It was more than I could take. Patty was different.

She wasn't a trained nurse or even one of those special workers who went to classes to aid the terminally ill. She was simply a regular volunteer, but one who had decided to spend each afternoon of her life with a book in her hand reading to me. She loved books, and I can remember looking at her for hours, seemingly without even blinking as she read. She would read all the stories I loved to hear with great expression. Sometimes she would cry or laugh to illustrate the story better. Every so often she would look up to see if I was still with her or if I needed anything. I never did. Her presence was enough to send the pain and fear fleeing into a special hiding spot for the moments that she sat by my side.

The mornings were the worst. Again I was served a meal, much to my disgust. Why bother? Sometimes my body would feel like it was being eaten from the inside out, with all the accompanying pain that went with that vision. Sometimes I begged to be released from what I knew was coming. I prayed to whoever would listen, crying out that I was weary of all this trouble and expense...then Patty would show up, and everything would change. We never spoke of my impending death. She treated me like I was going to spring up and run the next track meet any minute! There was never the pity that I so often saw in the eyes of almost everyone else that came in. I knew the names of her children and her husband, and even once got to meet them all. What a family! None of them seemed to mind that they were in the presence of a dying person—like they all took an angel course or something! Patty told me the secret later, and it was the only time she ever mentioned her spirituality or anything to do with God.

She told me that all humans have a path that is known to God and that somehow I was right where I had agreed to be, and with all of it there was honor for some reason. I laughed at her as I looked around at my surroundings and saw my bedpan, my half-full urine bag, and the tubes that were connected to my wrists. My eyes had grown more red with each passing day, and my complexion had turned to ash. I motioned with my tube-laden hand and said out loud, "Some honor, huh?" We had a good laugh, but she continued. She told me that she and her family believed that I had selected a special thing to do for the planet, and that my situation was somehow appropriate in the scheme of God's love. I didn't understand that at all, but it comforted me anyway. Hours after she left, I thought a lot about what she had said.

The inevitable happened, and I received a major answer to my most often prayed-for request. I had asked God (whom I never spoke to before I got sick) to let me go in the presence of my angel Patty—and I got my wish!

It was far easier than I had thought...this dying thing. Patty was just getting into my favorite part of *The Lord of the Rings* when my heart stopped. There was a moment of fear when I realized what was happening, and Patty stopped reading as

though I had sent her a mental message or something. She looked at me in a way I had never
seen her do up till now, and then I realized she
had seen this before. A faint knowing glint in her
eyes said, "Go peacefully in the arms of God."
She placed her hand on my chest, we looked at
each other in silence, and blackness took over for
a moment or two.

There was tremendous light! I was free! I felt a
grand release from my pain and began floating
above my body while watching everything in the
entire room. I saw my tired, frail body lying still
on the bed with Patty's hand still on my chest.
She closed her book slowly and remained still.
Only then did she cry a bit, but she shed tears of
joy at my freedom...and her countenance seemed
filled with honor for my life. I was watching the
whole thing!

As I gently floated further away, I saw her astral
wings and realized that just as I had somehow
honored the Earth with my passing, she was hon-

oring the Earth with her angelic service. Her body literally glowed with the role of who she was, as if there was a rainbow all around her head. My angel really was an angel...or at least an Earth angel! As the room faded, I realized that I hadn't told Patty that I appreciated her hours of service and work making my dying bearable. My gratitude towards her flooded over me...but perhaps too late! Did she know of my thanks for how she had comforted me? I was overwhelmed with emotion to think that the one human being who had helped me the most in my entire life had never verbally heard me tell her I was grateful. Then I saw the others around me and understood everything. I was peaceful now. She knew. Don't ask me how, but Patty knew. She knew how grateful I was even as I moved away. I saw her raise her open hand and lift her face to me as if she could actually see me! Was she waving? The surreal scene was beginning to fade, and my new surroundings were starting to take shape. It was time to leave.

❤ ❤ ❤

Patty sat for a moment silently next to the body, with her hand and face uplifted to the ceiling. She had been here and done this before. She felt the essence of life leave her friend on the bed, then she waited for a moment for what always came next. She was overwhelmed by a celestial wash of love. The feeling in the room was so thick that it was like a fog of warm mist that vibrated with the gratitude of multitudes for what she had done. This is why she seldom cried with sorrow at this moment, for how could anyone be sorrowful at such an honored event? Grieving for the loss would come later, but for now Patty sat in the place of honor for some time and celebrated the life of the one she had helped. No one came in, and she was alone to feel the love, thanks, and gratitude of all the heavenly entities in God's treasury that had gathered to lay hands on her. Patty understood what was happening and remained reposed and tranquil as she received her gifts of gratitude.

Feeling renewed, Patty slowly got up and gently covered her friend's head with the three-day-old sheet. She rose and began her walk to the hospital office where, that very night, she would receive the name of her next terminal patient—a person whom she would be with to read to until the end, when she would again receive the anointing of gratitude and the incredible wash of love energy from those heavenly beings responsible for such things. Patty understood that what she had just gone through was the closest any human being on Earth could ever be to God...and she rejoiced in the opportunity to do it all again.

I Love My Wall

Alan Cohen

__Alan Cohen__ is the author of ten popular inspirational books, including the classics, THE DRAGON DOESN'T LIVE HERE ANYMORE and I HAD IT ALL THE TIME. He is also a contributing writer for the bestselling CHICKEN SOUP FOR THE SOUL series. His column "From the Heart" appears in many New Thought newspapers and magazines. Alan presents seminars internationally and resides in Maui, Hawaii, where he conducts programs on spiritual awakening and visionary living. His latest book is called A DEEP BREATH OF LIFE: DAILY INSPIRATION FOR HEART-CENTERED LIVING.

❤ ❤ ❤

One Saturday after our excursion to Pizza Hut, the mall, and a movie, I drove my ten-year-old goddaughter Samantha to her family's new residence. As we turned off the highway onto a dirt road that led to her house, my heart dropped to see that she and her parents were living in an old school bus in a field.

As Samantha showed me around her family's quarters, I began to feel sad that this little girl whom I love so much was growing up in such a shoddy environment. As my eyes painfully fell upon rusted seams on the metal walls, cracked windows, and a leaking roof, I realized that her family had fallen into bare, subsistence living. I wanted to rescue her from such a barren plight.

Looking up at me with her big brown eyes, Samantha asked me, "Would you like to see my room?"

"Okay," I answered hesitantly.

The child took me by the hand and guided me up a makeshift staircase that led to a small wooden addition that had been superimposed over the roof of the bus. I shuddered to observe that her room was in the same condition as the rest of the place, just barely livable. Looking around, I noticed one fairly attractive element of her abode, a colorful tapestry hanging over the one section of the room that could be called a wall.

"How do you feel about living here?" I asked Samantha, waiting for a glum response.

Instead, to my surprise, her face lit up. "I love my wall!" she giggled.

I was stunned. Samantha was not kidding. She actually enjoyed the place because of this colorful wall. The child found a touch of heaven in the midst of hell, and this is what she chose to focus on. She was happy.

I drove home in a state of awe. This ten-year-old saw her life through the eyes of appreciation, and that made all the difference. I began to consider all the things in my life that I have complained about. I realized that in my preoccupation with what isn't there, I have been missing what *is* here. While focusing on rusty metal, I have overlooked some colorful tapestries. I made Samantha's statement my meditation: "I love my wall!"

Gratitude is not the result of things that happen to us; it is an attitude we cultivate by practice. The more we are thankful for, the more we will find to be thankful for. I heard of a woman named Sarah who lay in a hospital bed after an accident, deeply depressed, unable to move any part of her body except the little finger on one hand. Then Sarah decided she would make use of what she *did* have rather than bemoan what she was missing. She began to bless the one finger that could move, and she developed a system of "yes" and "no" communication with the little finger. Sarah became grateful that she could communicate, and she felt happier. As she blessed the movement, her flexibility increased. Soon Sarah could move her hand, then her arm, and eventually her whole body. It all started with the critical shift from complaining to blessing.

Harville Hendricks' book *Getting the Love You Want* has become a popular manual for relationships. The first step to getting the love you want is to *appreciate the love you have. The universe always gives you more of what you are focusing on.* Jesus taught, *"To him that hath, more shall be given; to him that hath not, more shall be taken away."* Jesus was elucidating a supremely important metaphysical principle, the very key to the manifestation of abundance. Jesus was teaching the importance of concentrating on what we have or want, rather than on what we lack or do not want.

We can look at any experience in two ways: through the eyes of lack, or the eyes of plenty.

Fear sees limits, while love sees possibilities. Each attitude will be justified by the belief system you cherish. Change your allegiance from fear to love, and love will sustain you wherever you walk. *A Course in Miracles* tells us, *"Love cannot be far behind a grateful heart and thankful mind ...These are the true conditions for your homecoming."*

The Gifts That Gratitude Offers Us

Lee Coit

*Nearly 20 years ago, **Lee Coit** began a quest for answers to his pain and frustration. He decided to devote an entire year to this search, and as a result, he discovered an inner guidance system. Since that time, he has followed this inner voice in making all his decisions. This path has lead to a peaceful and happy life, the writing of several bestselling books (LISTENING and ACCEPTING), and to giving lectures and workshops throughout the United States and Europe. For nearly ten years, he ran the Las Brisas Retreat Center. His dramatic change from a very busy advertising* *agency executive to a content and happy spiritual being gives hope to anyone who is seeking a better way to live.*

We think of gratitude as an appreciative word or deed given in return for someone's kindness. It was part of my early training to always say thank you even when I really wasn't thankful. Gratitude can become an automatic response to any situation that benefits us and is often given without awareness of its many benefits. Like Thanksgiving, thankfulness can become so stylized that its real meaning is lost. Just as "How are you?" is not a real question but a greeting, so "Thank you" can become no more than a nice way of ending an interpersonal interaction.

What gifts does gratitude offer us when we use it? A very old spiritual teaching says that "giving and receiving are the same." If that is so, what does being grateful do for us? First of all, gratitude has great restorative powers. Long ago, I found that being grateful for what I had helped me get over feeling sorry for myself. My appreciation of others always raised my own level of happiness. Whenever I thought I felt unappreciated, I'd count up all the wonderful things that had happened to me recently, and my joy would return. Being grateful for what I have is also an effective way of releasing a sense of loss. When I am aware of all the love I am receiving, I can quickly forget my problems. Gratitude is an excellent way of removing my concentration from negative situations and placing my attention on what is right. It doesn't matter whether I am grateful to my Divine Source or to my friends; the simple act of being aware of what I am receiving, and expressing my gratitude in action, brings the desired state of joy.

The second thing I noticed about being grateful was that I could extend my present joy backwards by holding thoughts of gratitude about people and events from my past. It always makes me smile, and my heart fills with joy when I reminisce fondly about my beautiful friends and the special times we've had. I've noticed over the years that the more gratitude I feel about the past, the happier I am in the present. Getting to a joyful state with gratitude is easy when I use pleasant memories, but I don't exclude unpleasant memories from my gratitude. Being grateful for those who we think have hurt us may be harder, but it is very effective for healing the past. I call this unconditional gratitude. *Unconditional* means that we give gratitude to everyone regardless of whether we think they deserve it or not.

What works for me is to remember only the good things about each person and let the other thoughts go. I can always find something about each one for which I am truly grateful. I have even started with the idea that at least these people are out of my life now. I then let go of my desires and plans for how they should have acted and try to think of one good quality they possess. Even if it is a small thing, I hold on to that thought and let the other memories fade. Once, for example, I started with the idea that when I had lunch with this person, we always went to a nice place. Daily, I bring this chosen person to mind and try to add one new positive quality. If I cannot add a new one that day, I go back to an old one. I do this until I can think of this person without dislike or a desire to avoid him or her. Before you know it, an amazing thing begins to happen.

At first I may struggle to find one little thing for which I am grateful, but as I keep trying, other good qualities slowly appear. They may not be qualities I like, but they are qualities someone else might like. When I continue to search for good qualities, after a while I begin to see how other people in my past have also benefited me. They may not have tried to help me, but my gratitude opens my vision to a point where I can see that they gave me a real spiritual gift. A real spiritual gift is something that increases my awareness of my true spiritual nature. It is all right if you never get to the point where you see these people as having helped you in a human or worldly way. It's all right that they never seem to change in the ways we approve of. It's important that you be honest with your feelings and not block out old hurts or pretend that everything is all right if it isn't.

To see the spiritual gift, I release my ideas of how I want things to be. It helps to ask questions of myself such as, "How did this person help me become more aware of my spiritual nature? How did their actions lead me or push me in a particular direction that benefited my spiritual growth? Even if the action was deemed harmful to my human and physical being, how did this action enhance and support my spiritual being?" As you can see, these are tough questions. There may be a desire to keep another locked in a web of blame and guilt. Unconditional gratitude given in these situations may at first feel as if we are letting people who we dislike "off the hook." I can assure you from my own experience that it is ourselves we are letting off the hook. Gratitude, like its sister, forgiveness, frees the giver first of all. Gratitude brings freedom to our self-imposed prison of hatred and revenge. Perceived past wrongs are our prison bars. Unconditional gratitude melts these bars away. Hatred not only locks us in a tiny cell of self-pity, it keeps out those who are seeking to bring love into our life. (Hatred includes everything from rage to a seemingly innocent desire to avoid someone.) Our past, released with gratitude, frees our present to be as it could be.

Finally, the most marvelous gift that unconditional gratitude gives us is clarity and vision. Giving unconditional gratitude, I begin to see that everything is here to bless me. I really cannot explain how this happens. It just does. It makes no sense in terms of our worldly thought processes. Only the actual act, in which you give gratitude unconditionally, brings the fantastic results of seeing clearly. As I keep extending my gratitude to everyone in my past and my present, I start to see that all that surrounds me is actually in harmony.

I begin to see that what I judged as harmful and unfair was really a misinterpretation, a faulty judgment based on my perception, which is very limited in its scope.

Human perception seems very powerful. It proceeds from our limited self-concept. From this view, that of a limited and unconnected being, we look out at a world filled with danger and pain. If we refuse to act on this perception but desire to see what is happening in our life spiritually, we get an entirely different view. We begin to see the interconnected and intersupporting relationships of reality. We begin to see the spiritual dance in which we are each engaged. It is important that you not try to figure out the dance, but merely let it reveal itself to you and then move to the beat. Unconditional gratitude, rather than seeking to control the situation, frees you from stress and pain. Unconditional gratitude replaces your frustration with the peace, joy, and happiness that is naturally yours.

The Circle of Gratitude

Terah Kathryn Collins

Terah Kathryn Collins practices, teaches, and lectures on Feng Shui, the Chinese art of placement, in San Diego. She specializes in teaching people how to see through their "Feng Shui Eyes," opening the vision that leads to living in optimal harmony, comfort, and balance. She is the author of THE WESTERN GUIDE TO FENG SHUI: CREATING BALANCE, HARMONY, AND PROSPERITY IN YOUR ENVIRONMENT.

❤ ❤ ❤

Expressing gratitude was something I learned by watching other people. At first, I wasn't very good at it. I often forgot or simply wasn't in the mood. Besides, I figured that people wouldn't notice if I wasn't grateful. It was like giving a gift they weren't expecting anyway. But on those occasions when my mood was just right, and I did grace someone with a sincere thank you, something magical always happened. A surge of joy would whip through my body, magnetically connecting me with the other person. I began to remember to be grateful more often.

I like to try different ways of expressing gratitude to see how they feel. Surprising people with a thank you is great fun—their faces always light up, and we laugh and hold hands for a moment. Gratitude sheds a rosy glow across my whole life. The more grateful I am for everything in life, the more reasons I find to be grateful. There are the big things, such as my "tribe," or my friends and family. There are the personal things, such as my good health and wonderful career. And gratitude reaches all the way down to the little things—the fresh flower arrangement, the bowl of oranges, the fire in the fireplace. Focusing gratitude on anything makes it grow!

Does this mean that because I'm grateful for the food on my table today, I'll soon be giving thanks for everyone around the community, the region, and the world having plenty to eat? Could it be that since I'm grateful for the peace that exists in my neighborhood now, I will soon have the opportunity to be grateful for peace on Earth?

I've decided that the answer is YES. The circle of gratitude gets bigger every day. One grateful thought and you're in. And once you are, watch the circle grow.

Gratitude—The Vital Ingredient in Our Lives

Dr. Tom Costa

Dr. Tom Costa is founder of the Religious Science Church of The Desert in Palm Desert, California, and is currently on the Board of Directors of Religious Science International. His popularity as a public speaker has resulted in a number of television appearances, as well as lectures and seminars throughout the United States, Canada, and England. Tom is the author of LIFE! YOU WANNA MAKE SOMETHING OF IT?

♥   ♥   ♥

My attitude of gratitude has been developing for the last seven decades of my life.

My deep feelings for the spiritual privilege of being grateful were tested when I first became a minister in 1974. I was counseling a man who was quite unhappy. Here was a man who was in good health, played tennis daily, was successful financially, and who loved his work. I had just performed the wedding ceremony for him and his new and devoted wife, and he also had a loving family from his previous marriage. Yet, although every area of his life—health, wealth, love, and work—seemed fulfilled, he was STILL unhappy.

As a new minister, I was stymied; what could I pray for? How could I help him move through his depression? As we continued our sessions, what came out was this man's lack of gratefulness. He never gave thanks for his health, his wealth, his children, his home, or life itself. He took every-thing for granted. This inspired me to find out more about this nebulous but vital ingredient in our lives...GRATITUDE.

How well I remember years ago when I was doing what is referred to as a Fifth Step in the Twelve Steps of the Alcoholics Anonymous pro-gram. The Fifth Step is the one where someone, perhaps a member of the clergy, would listen to an account of the alcoholic's life up to the time of admitting to their alcoholism. A young lady remarked to me, "You cannot be grateful and unhappy at the same time."

I was probably about 40 years older than she was at the time, but I was spiritually stunned. I had never heard that "one-liner" before, and it made sense! Since then, I have used that thought throughout my ministry—in classes, seminars, and in my personal life. YOU CANNOT BE GRATEFUL AND UNHAPPY AT THE SAME TIME. It is truly emotionally impossible to do both.

As I think about this concept, I flash back to my Catholic upbringing, where we used a rosary. Personally, now I have what I call a mental Rosary of Gratefulness. I count the "beads," if you will, daily and often in my morning meditations and prayers. This is when I count MY blessings, and not someone else's.

This period of gratitude in my life does not occur just on the third Thursday in November. This time of thanks is something I implement into each and every day. I have so many beads to count...beads representing people who have helped me...beads representing people who didn't help me (for this made me stronger in every area of my life). There are beads representing close, intimate friends, my family...beads representing my health, my body, my physical senses, my home that I treasure and enjoy. I give thanks for my pets, who teach me daily unconditional love. I give thanks for my ability to choose my thoughts, my attitudes, my path.

Take a moment of time daily, and be grateful for all that you are and for all that you are not. Be grateful for all that you have and for all that you do not have.

REMEMBER: YOU CANNOT BE GRATEFUL AND UNHAPPY AT THE SAME TIME!

Words of Gratitude

Sri Daya Mata

Sri Daya Mata is one of the earliest and closest disciples of Paramahansa Yogananda, author of the spiritual classic AUTOBIOGRAPHY OF A YOGI. She has served for the past 40 years as president of Self-Realization Fellowship, the international nonprofit religious society founded by Yogananda in 1920 to disseminate his universal teachings on India's ancient science of Yoga and its time-honored tradition of meditation. Soon after meeting Yogananda in 1931, Sri Daya Mata became a nun of the monastic Self-Realization Order; and for more than 20 years, Yogananda personally prepared her to carry on his spiritual and humanitarian work. One of the first women in recent times to be appointed spiritual head of a worldwide religious movement, Sri Daya Mata has made several global speaking tours, and she is the author of two anthologies—ONLY LOVE and FINDING THE JOY WITHIN YOU.

Gratitude is a quality that can contribute immeasurably to our happiness, for it is an essential aspect of love. Indeed, it draws us closer to the ultimate Source of all love.

Looking back on the many years that I was privileged to be in Paramahansa Yogananda's presence during his lifetime, I recall how often he encouraged us to cultivate the habit of appreciating all the good in life—not taking for granted even the little things. The more we express loving gratitude to God for our blessings, great or small, the deeper will be our attunement with that Infinite One, and our awareness of His responding love. And too, the divine laws of abundance operate more fully in our lives when we acknowledge and appreciate the Giver behind the bounty of our spiritual and material blessings. It is so rewarding to recognize the good in each moment, in every experience, looking to the Giver with a grateful heart.

How, then, do we cultivate such gratitude? One way is to dwell on some circumstance in our life for which we feel truly thankful. It does not have to be a momentous experience. A hint of some good done to us—maybe a smile that came our way and lifted our heart—is sufficient. Remembering such experiences helps us to develop a spirit of thankfulness.

As often as some sweet grace comes to you, inwardly say, "Thank You, my God." This simple practice brings far-reaching results, because to dwell on good is to magnify it. That which we enliven in our mind soon reflects in our outward behavior. Thus, a deep sense of gratitude ennobles our life and the lives of those with whom we associate.

Sometimes the greatest cause for gratitude lies concealed in the challenges we face, for they help to make us stronger and more compassionate human beings. The concept of giving thanks to God even in the midst of misfortune is a very beautiful one, often referred to in the scriptures of both East and West. More than that, it represents the truest perspective we can adopt. Even the highest and finest of the pleasures of this life are bound to come to an end. But God is our Eternal Well-Wisher, and when we turn to Him— whether in joy or sorrow—with a whispered word of thanks, we begin to transcend the fluctuations of earthly existence and to anchor our lives in a love that will endure forever.

Gratitude Is Awareness

Amy E. Dean

Amy E. Dean is an author and nationally known speaker on self-esteem, family relations, and recovery from a dysfunctional past. She has written a number of books, including PLEASANT DREAMS, LIFEGOALS, and FACING LIFE'S CHALLENGES: DAILY MEDITATIONS FOR OVERCOMING DEPRESSION, GRIEF, AND "THE BLUES." Amy currently resides in Maynard, Massachusetts.

There's a story of a spiritual teacher whose daily sermons were powerful and inspiring. Hours of preparation often went into creating such messages of hope, love, forgiveness, and joy. One morning, before standing to deliver the day's sermon, the teacher focused on the message about to be given and knew it would probably be the best ever. The teacher remembered the time spent writing and rewriting the words of hope and peace and felt confident that many would be touched by such wisdom. Smiling, the teacher arose and faced those who had gathered together for the day's message.

At that moment, a little bird came and sat on the window sill. It began to sing with a full heart for a few minutes. Then it stopped and flew away. The teacher was silent for a moment, then folded the pages to the prepared sermon and announced, "The sermon for this morning is over."

To me, this story reflects what gratitude is: being able to fully experience and embrace the spontaneity of a moment that's not sought after or anticipated. But how often do you allow that to happen? The mad rush of living, the mad crush of places to go and people to see, and the maddening stream of problems that need to be solved and conflicts that need to be resolved on a daily basis can make you forget that there's a world teeming around you with wonders.

Each day I need to remind myself that gratitude is awareness. My day begins with an early-morning run on dark streets. My concentration is often divided into many directions, from paying attention to the dimly lit road so I don't turn an ankle, to planning how my day will be organized. Before I learned about gratitude, I rarely took the time on my runs to notice the sky above me—still a night sky, with brilliant stars and an ever-changing position of the moon. But one morning, I happened to look up and, at that moment, saw a shooting star. The effect this fleeting instant had upon me was incredible. I smiled. I picked up my running pace. I looked around me and noticed other beauty—the silhouettes of trees presented against the indigo background of the sky, the way mica chips in rocks glistened in the beams from streetlights, the gurgling sounds that water made while running down a roadside stream. Throughout the day, I told my friends about the shooting star I had seen. And then the next morning I set off on my run ready to look down at the road, as well as to shift my focus from time to time to look around and above me.

Since then, I've seen two more shooting stars. I've also heard the screech of an owl and seen clouds pushed aside by gentle breezes. The way such sensual experiences make me feel inside reminds me of Alice Walker's writing in *The Color Purple*, when her character records in her journal: *"I've been so busy...I never truly notice nothing God make. Not a blade of corn (how it do that?), not the color purple (where it come from?). Not the little wildflowers. Nothing."*

How often do you take time to notice the wonders of the natural world on a daily basis—the rainbow after a storm, the birds frolicking around your bird feeder, or the silvery brilliance of a full moon? Gratitude is slowing down your pace, opening up your senses to the world around you, and feeling the impact such awareness has in how you feel and how you then live the next moment of your life.

Gratitude: One of Life's Miracles

Dr. Wayne W. Dyer

Dr. Wayne W. Dyer is one of the most widely read, internationally renowned authors today in the field of self-development. He has written numerous bestselling books, including REAL MAGIC, YOUR ERRONEOUS ZONES, STAYING ON THE PATH, A PROMISE IS A PROMISE, and EVERYDAY WISDOM; and has appeared on over 5,300 television and radio programs. He currently resides in Fort Lauderdale, Florida. This essay is adapted from Wayne's book YOUR SACRED SELF, published by HarperCollins.

♥ ♥ ♥

Expressing gratitude for the miracles in your world is one of the best ways to make each moment of your life a special one. As you progress on your path each day, have conversations with God in private and important moments. In these conversations, rather than ask for special favors, affirm your willingness to use all of your inner strength to create solutions. Ask for the inner wisdom to do so, and also give thanks to God for Her help.

Knowing that you are able to access divine guidance is more than a Sunday morning practice. It is a knowing that comes from within that can never be doubted or shaken because these moments translate to how you lead your life.

As you become more aware of the divine presence flowing through you at all times, you will find that you take more time to appreciate the beauty around you. As you contemplate a bird, a flower, a sunset, a mother and her nursing infant, a school bus of children, or an aged man, open your heart to them. Allow the love to circulate from you to them and feel it being returned. The more you practice receiving love from your surroundings, the more energized you will become.

There is energy in everything and everyone. The way that you receive this invisible energy is through the actual appreciation of the beauty and wonder of our universe.

With practice, you will be able to send out the love that you are receiving through the simple act of beauty appreciation. Try it!

Another positive result of being grateful for your world is your increased capacity to give. When you have gratitude in your heart, you will find a new willingness to give to others so that they, too, might experience the joys that you feel. You will find that you will want to contribute to the needs and wants of others without any expectation of acknowledgment.

But it is important to distinguish between giving and sacrificing. A sacrifice is generally *for* something. The sacrifice is only made to achieve something. When you are sacrificing, you are giving in order to get, and you are in an ego mode that programs you to believe that you are so important and special that you deserve something for your giving. Ego wants you pumped up and believing that giving indicates your superiority— as if your generosity sets you apart from others who are not as munificent as you.

Or, if you give because you feel that you have to, you are not authentically motivated by your higher self. It is the ego at work here, too, telling you that you are so much better than the recipients and that they *should* be grateful to you.

However, giving as a means of fostering intolerance and love through your sacred self is different. As you cultivate a sincere sense of giving, stemming from your own gratitude for the gifts that have been given to *you,* you will experience the notion that *giving is receiving* and *receiving is giving* in all its splendor. The experience of mindfulness of others' needs is one of the most blissful experiences that we can know. Recall how exciting it was giving presents to parents, grandparents, and siblings. The gratitude you felt for their happiness equaled, and may have surpassed, your own excitement about receiving gifts. Why? Because you were receiving when you gave.

You see, it is your sacred self that enables you to feel gratitude and to give unconditionally. It is your ego that wants a reward. But that is only because that is what ego knows as long as you continue to reward it for keeping you separate from your loving presence. Give your ego the experience of knowing the love and tolerance of your higher self, and you will automatically begin functioning the same way in your outer life.

The Meaning of
True Gratitude

Nicholas Eliopoulos

Nicholas Eliopoulos is an Emmy Award-winning producer, director, film editor, and sound editor, and the founder of the motion picture companies Earthlight and White Rock Entertainment. Nicholas directed VISIONS OF A NEW WORLD, which features Louise L. Hay, Ted Danson, and Dennis Weaver; and he spent over a year in Russia directing the TV special "Russia Today, A People's Journey." He has also worked on numerous feature films, including FOUL PLAY, NINE TO FIVE, and OUT OF AFRICA. A resident of Los Angeles, Nicholas is a member of both the Motion Picture and Television Academies.

❤ ❤ ❤

I have been, for the most part, a very grateful person all my life, but it's only been in the last few years that I've come to know the concept of gratitude in a larger, fuller meaning. I have lived what many people would call a "charmed life." I had a happy upbringing, a wonderful education, and I have found success in my chosen career. I have not achieved all that I have coveted as yet, and, like most people, I experience the pain and heartaches, the joys and exhilaration of this wonderment called "life," but I am fortunate that I possess many good and loving friends. I have much to be grateful for, yet one day I realized that there was something I didn't know: true gratitude.

The meaning of gratitude changed for me when I began to look at the "great force of all life"— beyond my taught perception of God. A dear friend of mine referred to that force as God/Goddess/All That Is. Up to that time, the concept of a Mrs. God was only familiar in the Goddess stories I was taught as a child about ancient Greece. My friend was talking about a "feminine force" that together with God gave "birth" to all material matter—our physical Universe. It wasn't until I took this concept (which is all "one" force) called God/Goddess/All That Is and examined it for myself, that my concept of true gratitude expanded immensely. I realized through this study that the feminine principle of the Goddess was first—that it was the Goddess who created, or brought forth, God, and together they created ALL THAT IS.

I know that this does not fit in with the chauvinistic, traditional religious view of God. Most of the world's religions don't even acknowledge a Goddess energy at all. And if they do, in whatever form, She definitely came after God Himself. The idea of the Goddess giving "life itself" to God, I had never heard at all, anywhere. Whether this idea is wrong or right, the product of just considering it suddenly gave me a whole new realization of what true gratitude must really be like. For the first time, I saw what I believed to be God's gratitude—His gratitude to the Goddess for His own creation.

I thought to myself, and I felt for myself, the immense scope of love and gratitude that God must feel. It was then that I truly realized that "life itself" is a gift. My life was, and is, a gift. The immense gratitude that poured out from this realization was colossal. I thought, If I could somehow feel the same gratitude for my life that God Himself had for His own gift of life, then everything I was, everything I did, everything I touched, would have a new and more special meaning.

Some people whom I knew back in my college days were cynical. They would say, "God is dead," or "God does not exist." I always felt that they were talking about themselves. That is, something within them didn't exist, and they knew it.

My favorite author, Ayn Rand, who wrote *The Fountainhead* and *Atlas Shrugged,* was often accused of being an atheist. But I saw her on TV once, and she said, "No, I am not an atheist. I shall never die. When I pass away, it is the world that will end...a beautiful world at that." She went on to explain, "On the contrary, I love the word *God* because it means 'the highest of the high.' *God bless you* is a wonderful phrase."

My dear friend Lazaris has said, "Life is a gift, and our job is to learn to receive it." For me, life is a gift, and gratitude is its magnet. With my friend's permission, I would love to end my thoughts with what Lazaris has expressed: "Gratitude is a tangible force. The more you feel it, the more reasons you will find to feel it. Gratitude is a miraculous force, like a magical magnet, generating and then attracting so much more than you have already received. It is like a living energy, clearing the way for you to become so much more than you have already experienced."

The Awesome Design of Life

James Eubanks

James Eubanks *is a successful author, national-ly syndicated columnist, and astrologer who con-sults professionally in San Diego. Raised in Birmingham, Alabama, James holds degrees in modern foreign languages and broadcast jour-nalism from Loyola University in New Orleans. Graduate studies in linguistics eventually led him to the West Coast, where he discovered the New Age and trained in a variety of highly specialized disciplines.*

❤ ❤ ❤

Expressing gratitude is my most natural inclination. As a child in rural Alabama, I was taught to be polite, generous, and grateful, always. When I became a man, I adopted this practice of gratitude and refined it into a more thought-out and examined way of life.

I've always seen myself as different. Over the years in dealing with this, I have come to appreciate why I felt this way. I stood apart from the crowd for many years, and while this was often painful, the experience allowed me to see others more clearly. Now I have perspective on the crowd even though I participate in its activities. Members of the crowd usually do not practice gratitude on a daily basis. If something good happens, they are grateful. If a bad thing happens, they definitely are not. Often, those who think this way are miserable, worried, upset, tired, strained, and resigned. We can choose to believe that the tragedy in our lives is fate acting against us if we want to. The powers that be will not argue with us.

And yet, there is another way.

Gratitude is an emotional response of love that wells up within when one is confronted by the awesome design of life. I enter the world each day with an expectant mind, searching for something to be grateful for and someone to be grateful to. Theology defines religious experience as a profound human awareness of a grand design. Gratitude is an access and a channel of consciousness that leads to this peace and understanding. It is religious experience lived daily.

Gratitude is not the same as relief. I am *grateful* for my life, the people I know, and my work. On the other hand, I am *relieved* that I am not sick. The first statement is based on what is true within me. The other is based on my fears and dread. We do not usually make this simple distinction. Relief implies that something could go wrong, but for the moment, all is okay. In practicing gratitude, however, you affirm that everything is already right and that nothing can go wrong. There is nothing to do, nothing to fix—for example, "I am grateful for my health."

Without a continual affirmation and prayer of thanks and appreciation, I find that my mind becomes bored, and my heart dulls. I withdraw from the world, resigned to my struggle alone. Gratitude is a way out of difficulty, pain, and isolation. In the face of adversity and distress, practicing gratitude requires us to give up our own ideas about what we think is happening to us.

There is always more going on than we are aware of in any situation, and this is what gratitude puts us in touch with. In the big picture, these difficult circumstances in front of me might be the missing piece of a greater puzzle that I'm not yet aware of. I must give up my fears and judgments that something has gone wrong. In principle, this always leads to awareness.

Gratitude is an access to awareness, and awareness is a doorway to love, unceasing. It is a turn of mind, a re-orientation, a commitment in consciousness towards love and acceptance of what is. We all can do this. We must only be willing. The practice of gratitude saves us from our painful human storyline, for it requires us to look deeper into our lives and the people around us. The surface rarely holds depth; rather, it obscures it. Gratitude enriches and deepens the colorful fabric of our lives by allowing us to see more.

It is impossible to feel worry, anger, depression, or any negative emotion of any kind in the presence of genuine gratitude. A beautiful sunny day and a dark, stormy day cannot occur in the same place at the same time. So does the practice of gratitude redirect our minds away from fear and toward the truth, clearing out all negativity, pain, and suffering. I have a preventive maintenance program for resignation, cynicism, and doubt. Every day, more than once, I search my mind for all that I have to be grateful for. Noticing the constant flow of prosperity, riches, and wealth coming toward me leads to a welcome and reliable constant: peace of mind.

So, if you are not yet someone who on a daily basis practices gratitude, like an unending prayer or background music for your life, I invite you to consider the possibility of doing so, beginning now. Come up to the higher room. Gratitude requires responsibility. See and begin to own your valuable contributions and talents. Acknowledge the people in your life: those you love and those you may not love. In a true sense, they are all the same. They are your teachers. Be grateful for them. While doing so, realize how powerful you are, how moving your life is, and to what extent you are blessed in just being here.

And then watch what happens.

Gratitude Feels Good!

Sylvia Friedman

Sylvia Friedman *has been an astrologer, human behavior consultant, and handwriting analyst for over 20 years, and has appeared as a guest expert on numerous TV programs, including "Oprah" and "AM Chicago." A resident of Chicago, Sylvia is the author of THE STARS IN YOUR FAMILY: HOW ASTROLOGY AFFECTS RELATIONSHIPS BETWEEN PARENTS AND CHILDREN.*

It's important to set aside time for gratitude. When you look into yourself and into your life, it may be easier to see the bad before the good! But remember: thinking negatively will bring down your self-confidence and will make difficult situations worse. Those of you who believe in the idea of self-fulfilling prophecies can understand that it's better to open your minds and hearts to the good things that can happen, rather than to the bad. I'm sure that most of us can remember the beautiful, simple moments in life, such as smiling at a stranger in the supermarket and receiving a smile in return.

Wouldn't it be wonderful if we could freeze those moments in time so that we could fully appreciate when someone squeezed our hand, shared a laugh with us in the movies, or sat quietly by our side to comfort us! Each day offers a reason for gratitude, and we need to look for those special moments and remember them. Good health, the ability to help others, and the support of good friends are all reasons to be grateful. Nothing in life should be taken for granted. Each day I personally thank my parents for giving me the freedom to make my own choices in life. Inner strength comes from holding on to the one person who can help you—yourself!

I have always been impressed with the song "The Best Things in Life Are Free." Gratitude is free—there is no cost. Nature's miracles, such as the flowers in bloom, the leaves when they turn bright colors in the fall, or the sky when it's blue, remind us of the simple pleasures in life. I remember a friend of mine who was going through a very sad time telling me: "I'm thankful when the sun is shining, as it gives me a positive feeling." I smiled and told her, "The sun shines not on us, but *in* us."

I wake up each day, and I'm grateful to hear my phone ringing because I know that it's one of my friends checking in to see that I'm okay. I thank God that I can look out my window at the lake and begin each day with peace. Many of us have similar opportunities, and it's so important to appreciate them. Those of us who have struggled to receive the good can be thankful that we have had the energy and strength to fight for what we believed in. If we have faith in ourselves, our own self-esteem will bring us to the place where we need to be. When our path draws us to the harder lessons in life, it's best to learn from them and move on. Hope, faith, and optimism give us the strength to hold on to tomorrow. Life can be a real challenge, but our dreams can come true if we are thankful for what we have already been given.

Finally, we can all be grateful for the courage that allows us to take personal risks, since believing in ourselves is the most important strength we have. We all have the ability to gather love, friendship, and knowledge before life passes us by. It's up to us to make the effort. Those of us who understand the importance of gratitude can encourage others to recognize their own special moments. *Gratitude feels good!*

Being Grateful During Life's Challenges

Shakti Gawain

Shakti Gawain is the bestselling author of CRE-ATIVE VISUALIZATION, LIVING IN THE LIGHT, RETURN TO THE GARDEN, AWAKENING, THE PATH OF TRANSFORMATION, and several other books. A warm, articulate, and inspiring teacher, Shakti leads workshops internationally. For nearly 20 years, she has facilitated thousands of people in learning to trust and act on their own inner truth, thus releasing and developing their creativity in every area of their lives. Shakti and her husband, Jim Burns, are co-founders of Nataraj Publishing. They make their home in Mill

Valley, California, and on the Hawaiian island of Kauai.

It is relatively easy to feel grateful when good things are happening and life is going the way we want it to. Even then, we often take things for granted. It feels so good to take a moment to express our appreciation to other people, to the earth, to our higher power, to life.

A much greater challenge is to get in touch with gratitude when we are going through a difficult time, or life is not going the way we think it should. At these times, we are more likely to be feeling hurt, confused, or resentful, which is perfectly natural. Gratitude is the last thing that would occur to us at such a moment. There have been times in my life when I felt more like shaking my fist at the universe, wondering why it was dealing me such a cruel blow.

It's interesting, though, that after going through a difficult time, in retrospect we can often see that there was something important and necessary about that experience. We may not arrive at this perspective until months or even years later, but eventually we can see that there was some important lesson learned, a deepening of our wisdom, an awakening, or perhaps a new door that opened in our life as a result of events that seemed negative at the time.

For example, the loss of a job may have led us to spiritual or emotional healing. The ending of a relationship may give us the opportunity to discover that we need time alone, or it may pave the way for a more satisfying partnership. At that point, we may begin to feel grateful that life unfolded as it did.

Usually, a painful time in our life is what I call a "healing crisis." We are letting go of something old, and opening to something new. Often, it happens because we have *already* grown in consciousness, and therefore can no longer live in the old way. Sometimes we are being confronted with a necessary change that we must make within ourselves and/or in our lives. There is a grieving process that we must go through as we let go of something we've been attached to. We must allow ourselves to feel our fear and sadness, and we can also remind ourselves that there is a gift in this experience that we simply can't yet see.

So if you are going through a healing crisis in your life right now, reach out for as much support and love as you can, and allow yourself to fully experience all the feelings that come up. Ask that the gift in this experience be revealed to you as soon as you are ready for it. And remember that after a little time passes and you gain perspective, you will once again feel grateful for the amazing journey of your life.

Gratitude Is a Sanctuary...

Michele Gold

__Michele Gold__ is the author of the beautiful coffee-table book ANGELS OF THE SEA: SACRED DOLPHIN ART OF ATLANTIS. Her award-winning spiritual artwork and storytelling reflects dream imagery, visions, myth, and the actual experience of swimming with families of wild dolphins. Her work has appeared in national publications films, and has been exhibited in private and corporate collections around the world. Possessing a deep love and respect for all of life, it is Michele's greatest hope that others will share her compassion for these exquisite dolphin beings. Michele is *a professional fine-art illustrator, writer, photographer, dancer, and musician who believes that love is always the answer.*

My father told me a wonderful story about a father who gave his young daughter a simple locket and told her that it contained a very valuable diamond sealed inside the locket, so if at any time she was ever in need, she could crack open the locket, sell the diamond, and make it through difficulties.

The daughter grew into a woman and struggled alone through terrible times of poverty, but just the mere thought of the diamond resting safely inside the locket she wore around her neck gave her enough courage to pull her through. Many years later, she had finally become a success in all areas of her life and no longer had to struggle for survival. Her curiosity had grown to the point that she had to know how much the diamond was actually worth.

The woman took her precious locket to the finest jeweler in the village to have the diamond appraised. The jeweler eyed the plain, tarnished locket with a bit of disdain, raised a mallet, and with one swift blow smashed the little locket into many pieces, releasing a small, shiny piece. The jeweler held it up to the light and said, "Why, this is not a diamond, my lady, but a worthless piece of ordinary glass!" Stunned by the news, the woman laughed and cried and then laughed some more.

"No, kind sir, that is the most valuable diamond in the world!" she replied, wiping the tears from her eyes.

Her father had given her a priceless gem...the gift of hope and the belief that she would always be all right, and for this she would always be grateful.

As I searched over the experiences I am most grateful for, my mind travels in a spiral. No matter how unique the experience, the center is always kindness. I was delighted to discover that the definition of gratitude is *the appreciation for kindness*. I strive to live my life as a practice based on gratitude. My first teachers were my parents, brothers, and all of the little bugs living under the moss garden in our tiny backyard. I remember understanding gratitude when a bright yellow skipper butterfly would light on my hand or when a wild bird would let me get close enough to see her feathers up close.

Gratitude is not always instantaneous. There are some things that take time to reveal what was gained, when there can be insight. Many times a lack of gratitude can be a powerful blow back on course. There have been many times that I have wandered too far from my heart and grown dissatisfied; these were signs that a change needed to be made, and that unhappy event became a turning point, a shift back in the direction of love and gratitude. As an adult, several encounters with wild dolphins further opened my heart and mind to the experience of unconditional love and appreciation for the present moment, for which I will always remain awestruck and grateful.

A wonderful meditation teacher taught me how to set intent. This is a way of creating a clear signal to the Universe about your direction in life. You set your course and then adjust the sails on your ship headed towards a sacred island, obscured by mist and miles, but your intuition knows it is there. You may be diverted by powerful, whirling winds, but set back on course by gentle tropical breezes. Night may fall again and again, and yet you hold deep inside a map guiding your mystic journey. Eventually, you will reach your destination if you continue to set your intent.

I believe that gratitude is the way we reach ourselves. Every morning and night, I focus for a moment and give thanks for the gift of my life and for the presence and love of everyone in it. I give thanks for all that I am given and all that I am learning. I give thanks for all that I wish to accomplish as though it has all been achieved. I offer thanks to all of the guardian angels and Nature Devas for their healing of loved ones and the planet. I ask for guidance and seek dreams for answers. I give thanks for good health and the richness of my senses. I give thanks for the profound beauty and magnificence of the Earth. I give thanks for the gift of creativity and the ability to express my feelings through paint, word, music, and dance. I am grateful for the wisdom, granted through ancient stories, images, and Nature, from centuries of yearning. I give thanks for the exquisite dolphins, birds, trees, and all that is living. I give thanks for the abundance and prosperity that is ever-present. And above all...I give thanks for kindness.

Many times, when my life was very painful and difficult, I was very grateful for many gestures of kindness. For years I felt alone in my struggle, and yet some part of me knew deep down that I always had a diamond. I have deep gratitude for the incredible gifts of love and life.

Always treat yourself as a precious, priceless being worthy of love.

Gratitude is a Sanctuary that allows us to love even deeper.

FULL CIRCLE

Swimming for thousands of years, under the many full moons...I searched for you.
Lost ships and lost souls land on warm places guided by yearning and the angels of the sea.
My heart wanders, I curl in and hold myself, longing for home,
not knowing it is always here.
And in the moving up and outward, of the pressing of the rain, breathing through my eyes,
I sense the coming sweetness, of many trees smiling in the knowing that

those treasures buried so very deep in my heart
have begun to sing the
Song of Angels Dreaming.
With my Soul as the only map,
with which to drive,
with which to guide
My wanting of the world to be smooth with the
gentleness of tender hands,
glide so silent, of sweet music of birds
curling from the deepest place...
I smile inside,
I smile deeply.

❤ ❤ ❤

Gratitude: It Can Make Your Day!

Karen M. Haughey

Karen M. Haughey *is an award-winning fine artist, poet, and designer whose work has been shown in private collections throughout the world. She is also the author of the coffee-table art book ANGELS: GUARDIANS OF THE LIGHT. When she is asked what inspires her painting of primarily angels and mermaids, she replies, "It consists of looking within one's self on a visionary level through means of meditation and comforting sounds, such as music." This, in turn, stirs and enlightens the creative intellect, thus avoiding* *preconceived logic. Karen makes her home in Northern California.*

♥　♥　♥

I would like to begin by expressing my own gratitude to my dear friend Louise L. Hay for making many of my long-term dreams become realities. Her love, support, and kindness will always leave me eternally grateful!

I am also filled with gratitude for my God-given ability to paint angels as I do. Because the gift that I have is not about me—it's for others and how it affects their lives.

Life is not meant to be isolated for one's self, but is meant to share in the context of love and peace. Gratitude also comes by virtue of doing for others, or what some would call random acts of kindness, for no reason other than just wanting to do a good deed for someone, whether it be a total stranger or someone you've known all of your life. I get complete satisfaction from doing these types of things. Not that I'm looking for it, but it always comes back to me, and I know that God is always watching!

I remember a few simple incidents, one when I was crossing the San Mateo Bridge, close to my home in the San Francisco Bay area. I always pay for the car behind me in the toll booth. Anyway, this very expensive car with the tinted windows and the works pulled up behind me. I gave the toll-booth attendant the extra dollar as usual and asked that the car behind me be paid for. She looked at me a little funny, since she was obviously comparing the status of our respective automobiles, but she did as I asked.

I rarely get a reaction from people when I offer this gesture, other than a smile or a wave or sometimes a strange look, but this time was a little different. The aforementioned car drove alongside me and rolled down its windows, and two young girls and their mom and dad started waving and honking with joy and excitement like I've never seen, with all of this gratitude and thankfulness we've been speaking of. You would think by their reaction that I had done a lot more than just pay their toll, and it's such a simple deed. But seeing the surprise and happiness on those children's faces and the element of disbelief on the parents' faces was enough to make anyone's day.

Another time, I was driving through a residential area and noticed that someone who was parked outside a home had left their car's headlights on. It meant going out of my way, but I turned my car around and walked up to that house, knocked on the door, and told the occupants that they had left the lights on in their car. The family living in that house thanked me over and over as if I had performed some miraculous deed, which obviously I had not, to my own thinking.

So the point I'm making is not what you can give on a tangible level, but what you can ultimately give from your heart and soul to another human being without expectation.

The gratitude you will receive will come by way of your giving it away.

Life is a gift, and what you do with yours is completely up to you. Be thankful for this gift, and use it to heal this beautiful planet we live on, our Mother Earth.

An Appreciation of Gratitude

Christopher Hills, Ph.D.

Christopher Hills, Ph.D., D.Sc., is the author of 27 books on consciousness, the former president of the World Yoga Society, founder of the University of the Trees (1972)—a pioneer in developing food resources from algae to alleviating world hunger—and founder of the Light Force spirulina company. He is presently engaged in projects for the homeless, and emotional literacy in children.

❤ ❤ ❤

I am most grateful when I have just had a close encounter with death. Once the front wheel flew off my Buick as I was driving down a steep, curving hill. I maneuvered it to the bottom of the hill in a shower of sparks and accompanied by a prayer. Another time I was deeply grateful when I was struck by lightning on the bridge of a ship that hit the upright stanchion two feet away from my face, and millions of volts of electricity were magically conducted to Earth through the steel into the ocean below. I gave thanks and have never forgotten the smell of burned air instead of burned hair.

When I was born, I was also struck by lightning inside my mother's womb. She was badly burned on her arm, and I came out suddenly with a big red birthmark from elbow to wrist that lasted 14 years. My mother was so traumatized that she could never hug me without feeling totally overwhelmed. I was too young then to be grateful for the gift of life. But in retrospect, I give thanks that we both survived this electrical charge, and I am still alive and kicking in the human world.

I can think of many instances of gratitude that did not come until after I had begun to appreciate all the goodness that life has given me. I know now to express that gratefulness—not only in times of peril, or greatest abundance—but for all that I experience. I am grateful not only for incredible friendships, but also for those who have been liars and deceived me, because of the many lessons of life that they have brought me, thus sharpening my appreciation of those who walk their talk and live up to their spiritual words.

One of my most grateful moments was when I came to after being knocked unconscious in a storm. I was on my yacht in the West Indies, taking guests around the island of Jamaica heading towards Port Antonio.

Louise Hay and her then-husband Andrew, who were, at the time, my partners in the spice trade, were among my guests on that trip. We got into a storm about a half day's sailing from Port Antonio. The big boom, over one foot thick, suddenly flashed right over in a freak wind and knocked me from the wheel house into the scuppers. The side rail of the boat was practically under water. Somehow I got stuck between the rails and was lying there unconscious, and I blacked out. The next thing I saw, after what seemed like an eternity, was Louise's face leaning over me and Andrew shouting at me and shaking me at the same time. He was saying I just had to wake up because nobody else knew how to sail the 90 tons of deadweight of this ship. No one knew the course to sail to Port Antonio, and we had lost sight of land.

This was one of my first experiences of being absolutely needed. Without me, Andrew was saying, we would all perish. As I regained consciousness and realized what he had said, I realized how some people are lucky to escape death, but there are those whose destiny can be strongly interwoven with another person's skills. I have never forgotten my feeling of relief when I found I could still walk and talk! I had to wait another eight weeks for my wrenched neck to stop hurting me, but all the while, I thought about how thankful I was to be alive and how lucky for my guests that I could navigate them safely to Port Antonio.

I can still see Louise's face as I woke up in the storm, with her makeup all washed off and her hair wet and dripping. I am even more grateful that 38 years after that event, life has made me even more grateful. I believe that I was protected by some higher power so that I could take a totally different course in life. I have no name for this power, although I have heard many. I prefer to feel it as a "Goddess Energy." This energy comes to us when we make room for gratitude and appreciation in our heart. It can also come to us as subtle intelligence moving through our natural environment. Within our consciousness, we reach outward to this intelligence, but really, its frequency and energy are hidden within.

Gratitude and appreciation taken all the way to the source of life comes when we surrender to its hidden intelligence. This Goddess Energy has been much forgotten and ridden over roughshod in our culture. In many other civilizations, it is repressed entirely with not even the dignity of human rights. Under different banners, they kill it by promoting "the one and only way to salvation." This is not the way we receive grace.

Ultimately, the feeling of gratitude comes from our attitude toward receiving. It is that form of appreciation that makes our gift have real worth. When we do not effectively "receive" a gift by not appreciating it, then the gift has not effectively been given.

The attitude of giving gifts is not greater than the attitude of receiving. It is much easier to give a gift than to truly receive one. Of all our natural talents, the precious gift of consciousness is more often taken for granted. How can we give to others in spirit what we have not fully received and appreciated in our own self? I believe in this case we must first receive gratefully that which we are giving to others, or our gift does not work.

I am grateful that I can find beauty and loveliness in life to shower my love upon and remain in bliss. Gratitude is knowing that all gifts have little value until they are fully received. In reality, it is our gratitude that gives real value to any gift. To be able to forgive all injuries is the greatest gift that we can bestow upon ourselves, but few are grateful for this choice.

If people don't appreciate where the power comes from, they are not going to get very much from its source. All gratitude is the result of this appreciation.

To choose consciously to forgive the past and any hurts that may come in the future is a gift you can never reciprocate because it dissolves all karma. To get home free without karma is only possible when we honor and appreciate the deep power of gratitude. In offering up our gratitude, we open ourselves to receiving and living in a state of grace. This is the gift of the Goddess, and she is longing to bestow it on us all. Being so grateful even before you receive—this is the stuff that creates miracles.

Gratitude:
The Key to a Happy,
Healthy, Successful Life

Sharon Huffman

Sharon Huffman, founder of the Center for Enlightened Leadership, teaches inspired leadership and true empowerment. She has been a consultant to leaders in every field all over the world. She coaches individuals in reaching their full potential and living in balance, while making a noble contribution to our world. She is a speaker, consultant, and author. Her work is included in WOMEN OF VISION, published by Nataraj; and CHICKEN SOUP FOR THE SOUL, by Jack Canfield and Mark Victor Hansen.

❤ ❤ ❤

This morning as I took my walk, I was filled with gratitude. The sky was blue, the temperature a balmy 74 degrees, and everywhere I looked there was beauty. Lush, breathtaking beauty—green rolling hills, flowers and palm trees, the sound of waterfalls and fountains, ponds filled with ducks, a stork in mid-flight over the lake, and magnificent snow-capped mountains. As I took in this opulence as far as the eye could see, I was overcome with gratitude.

I thought back to a time three months ago when I hiked in the freezing mountain snow and asked my spiritual source to guide me to a warmer, more beautiful place where I could take my morning walks. I remembered filling my heart with gratitude for all that I had been given, and almost without effort, I was gracefully led to this beautiful paradise.

In my 15 years of coaching clients to lead successful, happy lives, I discovered a secret. If I taught them to practice gratitude, everything in their life transformed. They felt good about themselves and were empowered to create the future they desired. The events in their life and their ability to respond in a positive way made a complete 360-degree turn. It was as if they had found a magic wand.

Gratitude changes the way we view life and ourselves. Difficult situations that were once intolerable and seemingly unchangeable, transform. The moment we feel gratitude, the situation begins to lighten, and then we can see the opportunities to create change. We feel better about ourselves and our ability to positively affect our environment and our world. Depression lifts, conflict turns to harmony, and stress releases to peace. When gratitude becomes a way of life, success, happiness, and health become the norm.

Whenever we feel angry, fearful, sad, or depressed, we have lost our gratitude. I can remember countless times when I felt resentful or down in the dumps and have chosen to count my blessings and feel grateful for all that I have. Almost immediately, I felt better. When we find something to be grateful for in a situation that has been troubling us, it uplifts and energizes us.

As soon as we feel gratitude, everything changes. It can transform a situation where you feel sadness and loss that, in turn, draws more sadness and loss to you, to one of joy and happiness. The *very same* situation is immediately transformed when viewed with a heart filled with gratitude.

In my own life, it has made all the difference in the world. I first learned the power of gratitude after the traumatic loss of my mate in a plane crash. After months of feeling despondent and close to despair, I was drawn to read the ancient wisdom where I learned that my life had meaning and purpose. As I began to feel gratitude, my whole life changed. First, my perspective shifted. Then I started to feel positive and empowered to begin again. Suddenly, instead of my life ending, it was a whole new beginning.

Shortly after that, I was diagnosed with a life-threatening illness and given six to nine months to live. As I continued to practice gratitude, I felt the disease being flushed from my body and my cells being flooded with life and vitality. I later learned that feelings of gratitude release positive endorphins throughout the body, creating health.

Gratitude not only heals, it rejuvenates the body. If you doubt this for a moment, just take a look at someone's face that has been ravaged by years of resentment. They will look drawn and haggard. Then look at someone who has lived their life in gratitude. They will be radiant with health and aliveness.

The key to a happy, healthy, successful life is gratitude. It uplifts us and sustains and draws to us what we want. Just as I did three months ago on a morning hike, when we focus on what we want with gratitude, we draw it to us. We become a magnet for our good.

When we give gratitude to life, life gives back to us. When we feel grateful, people, as well as the abundance of the universe, are drawn to us. If you have money problems and you find a penny, *feel* gratitude with great intensity, and you will draw more money to you.

When we give thanks for the situations and events in our life that are challenging, knowing that we are being blessed with wisdom from this experience, the very act of gratitude transforms the negative experience into a positive one. When we express gratitude, we draw to us people and situations to be grateful for. That is the magic of gratitude.

Gratitude fills our hearts with gladness and allows us to see the truth, empowering us to make the right decisions and take appropriate actions. With a grateful heart, we can see the best in every situation and everyone we meet, and bring out their best.

Gratitude is also a gateway to the Divine. A grateful heart is an open heart and continually lifts us higher until we connect with the Divine.

A few years ago, I took a trip to Mt. Shasta in Northern California in a desire to come into deeper communion with my higher self. During the long hours of driving, I placed my attention on my higher self with love and gratitude. Hour after hour, I raised my focus to just above my head, sending love and gratitude to this beloved part of myself for gently guiding and protecting me moment by moment, day after day.

In the last hour of the trip as I was entering the beautiful pine forests surrounding Mt. Shasta, I felt my higher self descend and wrap her loving arms around me. As this presence enveloped me,

I felt totally loved. It wasn't an intellectual idea; it was kinesthetic. I could actually *feel* every cell of my body being enfolded in love. Feelings of bliss washed over me, totally complete in this sacred union. I knew I was in the arms of the beloved.

In that moment, I understood what all the mystics have said down through the ages, that we are never alone. We are all connected with the Divine. Any thought that we are separate is an illusion. Love and gratitude reveal the connection.

This state of communion was the most glorious state I had ever experienced. During the night when I would awaken, I would immediately raise my focus to see if this presence was still there. Of course it was, and I would fall contentedly back to sleep.

As this state of communion continued, I found myself thinking that I had to hurry up to be somewhere. I would hear in my ear, "Slow down and be on time." This was very different from my usual way of hurrying to keep up with my schedule. But as I relaxed into this new way of being and allowed myself to be gently guided. I found that I always arrived at the right place at the right time. Life unfolded in an easy, effortless, magical way, filled with wonderful synchronistic events. It was like leading a charmed life with everything I needed brought to me. My conscious choice to send continual love and gratitude to my higher self was the key that opened the door.

It is always our choice how we want to live our lives. By choosing to maintain an attitude of gratitude, we are assured of living a happy, healthy, successful life.

"Gratitude Is Heaven Itself"

Laura Archera Huxley

Laura Archera Huxley *came to the United States from her native Italy as a concert violinist. In 1956, she married Aldous Huxley. She is the author of the books YOU ARE NOT THE TARGET; HIS TIMELESS MOMENT: A PERSONAL VIEW OF ALDOUS HUXLEY; BETWEEN HEAVEN AND EARTH, ONE-A-DAY REASONS TO BE HAPPY; and THE CHILD OF YOUR DREAMS, which she co-authored with Piero Ferrucci.*

♥ ♥ ♥

In the four words, "Gratitude Is Heaven Itself," William Blake, the mystic poet, expresses the essence of gratitude.

When gratitude begins at the time of birth, it becomes an integral part of our feeling life. Birth is a miracle, and it must be greeted with joy and gratitude. Unfortunately, this is not always the case. Too often, birth is surrounded by fear and unconsciousness. Yet, the fact remains that the marvel of physical birth is awesome—no less is the wonder of psychological rebirth, and of the physiological fact that the cells in our body are continuously dying and are immediately renewed with new cells. Often called a peak experience, rebirth is felt as freedom from ancient and constricting conditioning; rebirth reveals the wonder of the timeless renewal of life and of unexpected possibilities.

In our book, *The Child of Your Dreams,* Piero Ferrucci and I suggest a guided imagery of our ideal birth, *which can be experienced at any age.* Choose a quiet place to read your own ideal birth without interruption; it is a good idea to make your own recording of this meditation with your own chosen music, inspiring you with love and gratitude. Before you begin, breathe deeply and slowly a few times. Let each breath take you closer to that place in yourself that is untouched by all impressions, where the dramas of life have left no trace. There, everything is still possible, no thought is absurd, and everything seems to be happening for the first time.

Create Your Own Ideal Birth

Close your eyes, relax for a while, then let a vivid image of the place where you are going to be born to come into your mind. Look at this place, smell its fragrance, and let go of your present body. You're newly born, and you are very sensitive. You feel the vibration of love and gratitude all around you. There is a deep, natural peace in this birth, and you feel encircled by all the beings, real or imaginary, whom you love and respect. You have the whole creation ready to welcome you. You see your favorite flower, which, with its beauty and fragrance, tells you, "Welcome, I am grateful you are born! Welcome into the world, into the world of flowers."

Now look at the creatures, each welcoming you in its own language. It may be your favorite animal welcoming you into this world, perhaps a dog giving you a gentle lick or a dolphin with a miraculous flip or a butterfly with its fluttering wings—they all welcome you, saying, "I am grateful you are born. The world of creatures welcomes you."

Now you see the stars in the cosmos, twinkling everywhere. They, too, are speaking to you, saying, "Welcome. I am grateful you are born! Welcome into the world, into the world of stars."

You feel your entrance into a world that respects and welcomes you. You feel the gratitude of this world enveloping you. You breathe it so that it circulates in your bodymind. You feel this joy of entering life, of a welcoming world where you can do so many beautiful things, where you have the potential of giving love and evoking gratitude in others.

Now think of some of the great people in the history of the world—painters, philosophers, musicians, poets. Think of your favorite ones convening here to celebrate your entrance into the world. In their great knowledge, there is gratitude, also. Beauty, intelligence, and love are here, gratefully acknowledging your birth. You are a miracle, and everyone has come to tell you so. It has taken millions of years of evolution to produce You, a noble being with Godlike poten tial. Plants and flowers, animals and people, are all here to remind you, to tell you: "You are noble, you are beautiful, and we are grateful that you have come into this world." And in this birth there is joy. You see smiling faces, smiling flowers, smiling creatures dancing around you. The whole creation rejoices and is grateful to you.

You are entering a world where everyone is caring, a world where giving and receiving are just as natural as breathing. You are grateful for this new world. This gratitude is sinking deep into you, flowing into you, and becoming one with your own blood. Now your Soul and your Body know that...

Gratitude is heaven itself!

"Love Is the Way I Walk in Gratitude"
(A Course in Miracles)

Gerald G. Jampolsky, M.D.,
and Diane V. Cirincione

Dr. Gerald Jampolsky and Diane Cirincione are married and live in Tiburon, California. Gerald is a psychiatrist and founder of the first Center for Attitudinal Healing. Diane has been an entrepreneur with 25 years of experience in both corporate and private business. They are the co-authors of WAKE-UP CALLS, a book that reveals how we may achieve peace of mind by utilizing spiritual principles in all aspects of our lives. Their philosophy is based on concepts from A COURSE IN MIRACLES.

♥ ♥ ♥

"Love is the way I walk in gratitude" is a quote from *A Course in Miracles*. It is a walking meditation that we love to do with each other. Every step that we take we remind ourselves that Love is the way we walk in gratitude. And what beautiful peace and serenity it gives to us.

Another one of our favorite quotes is from Meister Eckhart, who states that the most important prayer in the world is just two words: "Thank you." It is our deep belief that everything that happens to us is a lesson that God would have us learn. Our lives become more peaceful when we stop interpreting everything that happens to us, and instead, experience everything that happens to us—no matter what its appearance—as a blessing in disguise. When we walk our pathway in life with a "Thank you" in our hearts, a "Thank you" in our minds, and a "Thank you" on our lips, whatever fear we may have been holding on to disappears, and the purity of love reappears. As we make the choice to lift ourselves up from the perceptual world and live in the world of God's love, "Thank you" becomes a way of life. The teacher that resides in our hearts would say that everything that happens to us in the perceptual world is but a new opportunity to choose the belief system of love, of God, a world where there is no form, just love.

By surrendering to love, by surrendering to God, we can go through each day acknowledging one another with gratitude. Imagine what the world would be if the only words we spoke, to God and to one another, were "Thank you." Each time we express our gratitude by extending our love to all, we believe that there is a little more light in the world and a little less darkness.

How quickly our world changes as we learn to return all the love that is continuously given to us by our Source. What greater gratitude can we give to our Creator than choosing to love one another and ourselves by seeing the face of God in everyone and knowing that it is a reflection?

There is a prayer that Jerry wrote some years ago
that we both like doing in the morning.

IN GRATITUDE TO YOU

My whole being pulsates
with the fire of desire
for our everlasting union.
My very breath is but Yours.
My heart is a limitless beacon
of Your Love.

My Spirit, being Yours, is the Light of the World.
My eyes but radiate and reflect
our Perfect Love.
My very essence vibrates with You as the
harmony of music not yet heard.

My vision, being Yours, can only bless.
My prayer is but an eternal song of gratitude,
that You are in me, and I am in You
and that I live in Your Grace forever.

Noticing the Abundance

Susan Jeffers, Ph.D.

Susan Jeffers, Ph.D., has helped millions of people overcome their fears and move forward in life with confidence and love. She is the author of FEEL THE FEAR AND DO IT ANYWAY, OPENING OUR HEARTS TO MEN, THOUGHTS OF POWER AND LOVE, and END THE STRUGGLE AND DANCE WITH LIFE, among other books. As well as being a bestselling author, Susan is a popular workshop leader and public speaker and has been a guest on many radio and television shows. She has also created many audiocassettes on fear, relationships, and personal growth.

♥ ♥ ♥

When I worked with the poor in New York City, I was always amazed at the gratefulness in the hearts of so many who, in a material sense, had very little. What were they grateful for? They were grateful to be alive, to have food on their table, to enjoy the sun on a beautiful day, to have their health, their friends, their family, and to be a contributing member of their community.

At the same time, I was always amazed by the lack of gratefulness in the hearts of so many who, in a material sense, had so much. If you were to ask me which of the two were happier, without hesitation, I would say the poor with gratefulness in their hearts.

What I am talking about here is very simple:

When we focus on abundance, our life feels abundant; when we focus on lack, our life feels lacking. It is purely a matter of focus.

It is true that we can't be in denial about the pain in our life. That is damaging to our physical and emotional health. And just as importantly,

We can't be in denial about the
abundance in our life!

I suggest that you create a "Book of Abundance" for yourself. Each night before you go to bed, jot down at least 50 wonderful things that happened to you that day. "Fifty things, Susan! I can hardly think of three!" Obviously, you have not been noticing the blessings in your life! The purpose of this exercise is to help you do so. Some of the items you can include are:

My car started • I am able to walk • I have food to eat • Someone paid me a compliment • My kids haven't gotten into any trouble today • I felt the sun's warmth on my face • I spoke to one of my best friends • The flowers are starting to bloom • I have hot water in my shower • I'm breathing • The sun came out

The items in your Book of Abundance do not have to be splashes of brilliance. In fact, it is better if they are not. Always keep in mind that if we focus only on the splashes of brilliance, so much of our life will seem drab...which it definitely is not! Take breathing, for example. Isn't it incredibly, wildly extraordinary?!

In the beginning, finding these 50 things to be grateful for may take a LONG, LONG time. Soon, however, the blessings will pour easily onto the paper. That is because you will spend much of the day LOOKING FOR the blessings in your life so that you will have new material to add to your Book of Abundance that night. And you will find them! The benefits are obvious...

As you start looking for the good,
your focus automatically is taken off
the bad...and you feel blessed!

If you can make noticing the abundance a habit, your life will be transformed!

I remember sitting with my mom in her living room on a cold, dreary winter day just months before she died. She was in much pain and was feeling very weak. At one point when I was in pain about her pain, she looked at me and said, "It's cold outside...I'm warm and cozy inside. My daughter is here...sometimes you get lucky."

Wow! I was focusing on her pain. She was focusing on her blessings. Thanks, Mom, for that beautiful lesson!

"In Everything Give Thanks"
(I Thess. 5:18)

Ione Shockey Jenson

Ione Shockey Jenson is a counselor, dream therapist, and teacher who holds degrees in education, psychology, and counseling. She is the co-author (with Julie Keene) of WOMEN ALONE: CREATING A JOYOUS AND FULFILLING LIFE. She is also the author of the self-published book EMPOWERING THE CHILD FROM WITHIN: EDUCATION AND PARENTING FOR THE TWENTY-FIRST CENTURY. For the past several years, Ione has been conducting workshops and doing private spiritual counseling. She is co-founder of the

Holo Center, a retreat community in Hayden Lake, Idaho.

♥ ♥ ♥

Learning about and understanding the concept of gratitude has been a lifelong process. I was fortunate to be born into a family who believed—even though times were hard and we didn't always have much in the way of worldly goods—that if you were grateful for what you had, God would always provide the rest. And, of course, we always had what we needed plus a little more that could be shared.

Both my ideas and understanding of the concept of gratitude have grown and expanded through the years. As a child, sitting between my parents in church on Sunday mornings, I often heard these words read from scripture: *"In everything give thanks!"* And my young mind responded with: "Yes, one needs to be grateful for every good thing that happens in one's life." From time to time, through the years of my youth, those words replayed in my consciousness, and I learned to be grateful for many obvious things. I expressed gratitude for gifts received, kindnesses bestowed, educational opportunities not anticipated, and all the good times and friends I experienced in the course of living.

As a young farm wife, I learned to be grateful for wondrous and simple things, such as the cooling rain that came down on a hot summer's day to give our thirsty crops the moisture they needed so badly. And, one year, after a sudden thunder- and hailstorm devastated our corn crop, I was even able to feel gratitude for the meager crop insurance that would help us survive our loss and enable us to stay on the farm another year.

It was easy to be grateful when, as a young mother, I sent joyful and unbounded thanks for the precious gift of my children. It was with an overflowing heart that I cared for them and watched them grow and eventually develop into the beautiful men they have become. My life was filled with gratitude for the warmth and closeness of our family. There were always so many things to be appreciative of, and I have often offered sincere prayers of gratitude as I counted my blessings.

As an educator, I took great pride and joy in my work and was always grateful that I could labor at something I loved, something that could make a difference in the world. I was grateful that I could touch the young lives of so many children and be the recipient of so much love and so many unlimited opportunities. I did indeed feel blessed.

"In everything give thanks." Then, as it sometimes happens, one day (21 years ago) while browsing through a bookstore, my eyes caught a glimpse of a book with an intriguing title: *From Prison to Praise,* by Merlin Carothers. This book introduced me to an intriguing idea. The author expressed the conviction that giving thanks in

EVERYTHING meant being grateful for all things—good and bad alike. While the concept was a novel one to me, the case made by Mr. Carothers was convincing, and I decided to try it out. Not surprisingly, I discovered a new dimension of gratitude and found that there was power in giving gratitude, even during the "bad times."

Expressing gratitude even when things went wrong was much more difficult to do, but I was also amazed at the outcome of doing so. I discovered that the scripture *"God inhabits the praise of His people"* was to remind us that gratitude releases an energy that could begin turning things around, and when I did so, it imbued me with the strength and ability to surmount whatever was happening in my outer world. Eventually, I would see that what had often appeared as a negative circumstance was really the pivotal point for a new direction that I would take. Often, in retrospect, I could see clearly that it had been a blessing in disguise and had led me into a deeper and more meaningful place.

In the years since discovering that wonderful aspect to thanksgiving, I find that being grateful for each new day as I awaken fills all my days with anticipation as I look for the blessings all around me, and as one by one, they unfold in magnificent synchronicity. Each morning, I bless my body for being the "outermost layer of my soul" and for serving me so efficiently and well as I move through my life's lessons and pleasures. I am grateful for the friendship and cooperation that my body and I enjoy. Many years ago, I began using my daily newspaper as my prayer list, and as I pray for those whose stories are written across its pages, I find much to be grateful for in my own life.

I have been a student of dreams for many years, and occasionally my psyche bypasses the symbolic process, and I awaken with a word message—a sentence or two running through my mind. I immediately write the message down lest it be forgotten, and one morning I awoke with the words, "Proceed through your days in an attitude of gratitude." As I pondered the levels of meaning inherent in those words, I realized that gratitude can be an act of will as well as an emotion or feeling. Gratitude can become a chosen lifestyle.

"In everything give thanks!" Now, I can be equally in awe of, and grateful for, a coastal sunset or the learning process inherent in an illness or a time of confusion. I can be grateful for my unshakable faith in Divine Order as my child faces a life-threatening illness over which I have no control, and in which I have, as yet, to fully discover all the lessons and meanings it holds. I am grateful for the times of connection with those I love, and I am equally grateful for the times of disagreement and estrangement that mirror for me new lessons to learn and insights to be discerned. I am truly GRATEFUL for discovering the power of gratitude in my life, and I shall always continue to give thanks in EVERYTHING!

Grateful Is Good

Elizabeth A. Johnson

Elizabeth A. Johnson is the author of AS SOME-ONE DIES: A HANDBOOK FOR THE LIVING; and is co-author, with Lucia Capacchione, of LIGHT-EN UP YOUR BODY, LIGHTEN UP YOUR LIFE. She has produced music, dance, and theatrical performances throughout the United States, and also promotes numerous arts-in-education programs. A long-time student of Eastern and Western movement and philosophy, Elizabeth is a certified T'ai Chi instructor, as well as a jazz and tap dancer.

♥ ♥ ♥

I am not fond of snow.
Cold wet winds neither
exhilarate nor enthuse me.
To praise with joy the glory of
harsh winter
would be—for me—
to sing a lie.

And yet

What graceful glory, serenity of silence, as the full
fat moon sends tiny beams to reflect on
snowflakes resting, like bridal lace, on the arms
of great trees. The absolute stillness of mid-
winter's eve unites above with below in such perfect symmetry that my heart swells, and I almost
cry at the deep beauty, deeper quiet, deepest
Oneness of it all. Thank you.

I am not particularly pleased
with things that slip and slide about
on ice—

like cars and feet—
or single digit temperatures
on either side of zero.

And still

I thank Beauty Blue—my car—and the fine folks who produced her Die Hard Long Life battery; along with most sincere, incredibly sincere, really truly sincere, appreciation to whoever invented car heaters. And, in the like line of motion, I take a moment to thank my feet for dancing (tap tap tap), and I send a warm wish to every winter dancer who de-ices a path to the studio door and bundles up for the warm-up. I thank T'ai Chi for everything!

My spirit does not gleefully jump at
soggy mittens, wind weepy eyes, cold ears,
red nose, almost frozen fingers and toes,
icicles forming in my hair, or
leaving my gloves in the car
overnight.

And also

Happily I extend heartfelt gratefulness to: soup, fuzzy slippers, a big bathrobe, ear muffs, gospel choirs with clapping hands, the sun, spring floral potpourri, down comforters, snooze alarms, hot water, the fireplace, bright blue skies, red socks, the good idea of dressing in layers, the sun, flannel sheets, my dog who climbs snow drifts and my cat who does not, hot tea with milk, leg warmers, friends in big sweaters, the sun, sheep who share their wool, snow men/women, new winter haircuts and Lady Clairol, the sun, toddlers toddling in snowsuits of color, a hot toddy, boots, flowers of any kind, and, oh yes, the sun.

It is not terribly thrilling for me
when parts of life are closed or canceled
like school and work, all dance classes, and
airports, roads, the grocery stores, the gas station.
Snow. Snow. Shovel. Snow.
Scrappy little snowflakes!

And so

Auriel Rose, my angel, giggles as I turn to the window and see laughing teenage neighbors snow-blowing my driveway and the mailman in hip boots maneuvering his route, singing loud and clear. I am reminded that God loves to smile. So I sit in my kitchen, crystal-induced rainbows flitting on the walls. Nothing to do today. The snow is quite massive. There is nowhere to go. Nothing to do today. What a concept! What fine fortune! Nothing to do today. So I think I will today! Think about many things today. Past-present-future things. All connecting things. Big, little, loving things. The Universe and me things. Way upstate New York things and Christenstaad, St. Croix things. Happy things, reflective things. Thank you—thank you—thank you things.

And when the moon, my sister, is brilliantly high in the sky, Auriel Rose and I will visit outside, and each of us will make one perfect snow angel.

That will be the wonderful winter thank-you note.
*Then all can see our gratitude and how joyful
it is.*

Great Days

Patrice Karst

Patrice Karst is the author of the book GOD MADE EASY: A SIMPLE GUIDE. She has been a writer and spiritual seeker most of her life. She speaks to audiences about the wonder of bringing God into their lives in whatever form they feel comfortable with. She lives at the beach in Los Angeles with her son, Elijah, where they enjoy hiking, ice cream parties, and gazing at shooting stars.

As the mother of a small child, I have often found myself suffering from the "poor me" blues. Raising a child alone is the greatest challenge that

I have ever been confronted with—emotionally, physically, and spiritually. When the loneliness, fear, tedium, and exhaustion have had their say, it can get really old. And, no matter how much I've told myself that compared to most of the other six billion souls on the planet I lead a charmed life, I realized recently that I still wasn't getting to that state of peace I desired.

So, I came up with a project to get busy and take my focus off my struggle. Each night before I fall asleep, my ritual is to thank God for something that has occurred during the day, something I am truly grateful for. Well, guess what happened? A miracle! I find myself walking around in a state of grace and gratitude most of the day. And, as my mind goes through the day searching for its "homework assignment," I can see just how many precious events occur during each 24-hour period.

From the most simple moments, such as the sound of my neighbors' wind chimes tinkling in the breeze, to the kind smile on the gas station attendant's face, to the warmth in my heart when my son Eli runs in from play just to tell me he loves me "bigger than the ocean, sky, and a hundred trillion moons," I now seem to have a long list each night!

I remain in awe (and profound relief) that no matter how overwhelming and scary this journey called "life" is, when I slow down enough, I realize that it's all just made up of hundreds of thousands of "moments," most of which are pretty darn wonderful if I just take the time to witness and appreciate them.

May we all remember to see and feel the Divine in everything—from a cool iced tea on a balmy day, to the warmth of the blankets that cover and comfort us all night. And may we pay attention to all the miracles that truly do dance all around us when we have the eyes to see and the ears to hear.

Bless It All!

Julie Keene

Julie Keene was formerly a professor at Ferris State University in Michigan, then went on to serve as a minister in Unity churches throughout the country. She is the co-author (with Ione Jenson) of WOMEN ALONE: CREATING A JOYOUS AND FULFILLING LIFE, and has also authored an autobiographical work called FROM SOAP OPERA TO SYMPHONY. She now works and lives at the Holo Center, a retreat community in Hayden Lake, Idaho, where she conducts workshops with a focus on spiritual and psychological growth.

♥ ♥ ♥

Gratitude and trust are closely related. In order to be thankful for everyone and everything in my life, I need to trust that the Universe makes sense, that everything my soul has chosen to experience this lifetime has been for my ultimate Highest Good. I trust that when it appears I'm failing, I'm only learning. I make a great effort to bless my life just as it is, both the so-called triumphs and disasters. A line from Kipling's poem *If* often comes to mind: "If you can meet with triumph and disaster and treat these two impostors just the same."

When I remind myself that I am a student in Earth School choosing those lessons that enhance my soul's purpose, it's possible to more readily bless every circumstance of my life. Of course, from a more unenlightened segment of myself, I sometimes wonder, "Why did I choose this particular misery?" Yet, gratitude for, and trust in, the ultimate justice of the Universe is the best antidote for the poisonous emotions of self-pity and resentment. I find it impossible to experience gratitude and negative emotions simultaneously. Author Elisabeth Kübler-Ross reminds us, "Should you shield the canyons from the windstorms, you would never see the beauty of their carvings." I've learned to bless and give thanks for the windstorms that have shaped my life.

When my soul arrived in Earth School, it set up some challenging lessons. Many years went by before I learned to see the blessings in these experiences. When I could honestly begin to understand their purpose and to feel gratitude for them, I made an escape from the darkness of a victim's prison into the light of freedom and joy.

Although "illegitimate" was stamped on my birth certificate, I am grateful I now know God has no illegitimate children. I acknowledge God's indwelling presence and embrace my innate worth as I go about completing my legitimate Earth School assignments. Although I was physically and sexually abused as a child, I am grateful that I now know my Spirit is indestructible and cannot be harmed by anything done to the Earth Suit. Although I've experienced "failed" relationships, I'm grateful that every relationship presents unique opportunities to practice love and forgiveness, opportunities to learn about myself at deeper levels. I'm grateful that it's possible to learn from relationships after they are over.

My oldest son Richard died when he was nine, and I'm so very grateful that I know that each soul chooses its Earth School experiences, including the manner and time of departure from the Earth plane. In Reality, there is no death; the soul is ageless and eternal, and love knows no barriers of time or space. My second son Robert nearly died when he was two and suffered brain damage as a result of the illness. I am grateful that I know that Robert chose this Earth School lesson, and as his mother, that I chose the experience with him. I've felt much pain watching him struggle with life, but he has demanded from me, and thus has taught me, unconditional love. Such a great gift!

Looking back over my life, I can see the beauty that the windstorms have carved. I trust current and future challenges to facilitate additional soul growth. My heart is filled with gratitude for all the people and events in my life because I now understand their Higher Purpose. My heart over-flows with gratitude for the Divine Love that enfolds, guides, protects, and sustains us all!

Gratitude: One of Life's Most Important Lessons

Kimberly Lockwood

Kimberly Lockwood *is a traveler on the spiritu-al path whose sunny, positive outlook on life makes her an inspiration and role model for her family and friends. She is most grateful for her role as wife and mother to Barry and Brittany Lockwood, respectively. She is the personal assis-tant to Louise L. Hay, and credits her family, Louise, and the Church of Religious Science as important catalysts for her own growth process. She is a resident of La Costa, California.*

♥   ♥   ♥

Gratitude is one of life's most important lessons. It can also be one of the simplest, if we learn it the first time around.

As a child, when I said thank you, I was saying what my parents had taught me to say. I did not have that true feeling of gratefulness. It was just something I did; it was what my parents called "good manners."

As I grew, this practice just became a good habit: "Always be polite, always respect your elders; always say 'Please' and 'Thank you.'"

As an adult, I began to appreciate the things around me—how beautiful the mountains are in the fall, the snow-capped peaks in winter, the vibrant colors of spring flowers, and how fresh and clean the air smells after it has rained. I started to see the beauty in the world around me. Was this gratitude I was feeling?

Time went on, and I enjoyed life and what it had to offer. I found the most wonderful partner. We became friends and then grew to love each other. We went through some tough times, but we grew stronger as a couple as a result. A year or so later, we were married.

Everything was wonderful! It was now time to settle down and start our life together. But instead, we went a little crazy for a while, just doing whatever we wanted, whenever we wanted. If we wanted something, we bought it. It didn't matter whether we had the cash or not; we simply charged it.

After a while, we stopped and looked at what we were doing to ourselves. It was not a pretty sight! Where did our gratitude go? We were taking things for granted, not appreciating what we had. Just wanting more, more, more.

Okay, time to straighten ourselves out. We started a savings account, only paid cash for things, and stopped going overboard with gifts. Family and friends will love us no matter how much we spend on them, we realized.

Times were very tough while we dug ourselves out of our financial hole. So, I can tell you that I am really excited to have a little cash in my wallet these days!

As time went by, I became pregnant—a wonderful surprise to my husband and me. As the months passed and that little life grew inside of me, so did our gratitude. Being able to experience this miracle was the greatest gift we had ever been given.

On the day our daughter was born and she was handed to my husband, I have to say that watching his face was incredible—his eyes filled with tears of joy. You could see the love he was feeling. Then, he placed her in my arms, and all I could say was, "Thank you, God!" Tears streamed down our faces. We had truly been blessed. As I looked into my daughter's eyes, I was completely overwhelmed with love and gratitude. She was an angel from God.

I finally got it—the ultimate feeling of gratitude. I carry that feeling with me every day. Gratitude is a special gift. Don't take anything for granted. Love and appreciate everything in your life. It's there for a reason—learn from it.

And remember, when you say thank you, really feel thankful. I do!

So Many Blessings

Sir John Mason

Sir John Mason was born in Manchester, England, in 1927. He was educated at Manchester Grammar School and Cambridge, where he graduated with a Master of Arts in history. He served in the British Army during World War II and the Korean War, where he reached the rank of Captain. John served in the British Foreign Service from 1952 to 1984, serving in Rome, Warsaw, Damascus, and New York. From 1976 to 1980, he was British Ambassador to Israel; and from 1980 to 1984, he was British High Commissioner to Australia. He retired in 1984 and settled in Australia, where he has been chairman of many large companies. He is a dual

British-American citizen. In 1954, he married Margaret Newton, and they have a grown son and daughter. John was knighted in 1980.

I am 68 years old, and I have nothing in my life not to be grateful about. I'm grateful to all the people who have given me so many reasons to be grateful. I have so many blessings that I lose count of them.

I will first try to count some of my personal blessings and then those that I share with others in the world.

Personal Blessings

My parents gave me high intelligence, motivation, and a secure and happy home. They encouraged me to win the scholarships, which, thanks to excellent teaching, paid for my education.

It may not be politically correct to say so, but I count myself fortunate to have been born heterosexual because...the greatest blessing of my life has been 40 years of marriage to a wonderfully patient and loving lady, to whom I am, of course, endlessly grateful. I hope I remember to tell her so. She gave us two admirable children, who are not only happy and fulfilled, but also on speaking terms with each other and ourselves.

Twenty-nine years ago, both of my lungs were covered with metastases (secondary cancer) following the removal of a kidney tumor. I was told that I had less than a year to live. My informants were mistaken, but to show they were willing, they gave me an experimental drug that they said could not harm me, which I still take every day. I am grateful to those who produced it, even though I am the only person in the world who has survived the treatment for more than five years.

But I am also grateful for the intense anger that my condition induced in me, and which, I am sure, was influential in defeating my lung cancer.

If I did not have two titanium hips, I would not be able to walk. Nor would I be able to see if I did not have two post-cataract intra-ocular lenses. Thank you to those who made this possible.

Shared Blessings

In the 1930s, as a young boy, I remember two friends dying of scarlet fever and diphtheria. Unknown now, I remember how everyone had one or two circular scars on their upper left arm: vaccination against smallpox. It has been fewer than 20 years since a vaccination certificate has been essential for overseas travel. Yet now, *smallpox, the greatest killer in history,* has been eradicated. Not so much a cause for gratitude, or a blessing, as it is a miracle.

I remember the scourge of tuberculosis: not a romantic disease, as with Keats and the Brontës, but a dreadful scourge, socially and medically. It has now virtually disappeared, and our gratitude is owed to those who accomplished its elimination.

I remember not being able to swim at the local pool for fear of contracting *polio!* Remember polio? Let us be grateful to Dr. Salk.

Let us be grateful that we can now talk openly about cancer, where 30 years ago it was a taboo subject. Because we can now discuss it, we get treated earlier and more effectively. I am grateful to be able to tell cancer patients of my history and to encourage them to know that there is hope.

Above all, as a father, I am grateful that my son has not had to learn to kill his fellow men in war, as both I and my father had to do.

It will be clear, I hope, that I believe that *the world has become a better place during my life-time,* and that I am lucky to have lived when I have. I am deeply grateful to those of my fellows, whether I know them or not, who have caused this to be so.

Gratitude:
A Healing Attitude

Emmett E. Miller, M.D.

Emmett E. Miller, M.D., has had more than 25 years of success teaching people how to enhance their health and well-being. His relaxation and imagery cassettes (I AM, LETTING GO OF STRESS, and HEALING JOURNEY, among others) are the accepted standard throughout the world and are in widespread use by Olympic athletes, business leaders, physicians, and others in the healing arts. His new book is called DEEP HEALING: THE ESSENCE OF MIND/BODY MEDICINE.

❤ ❤ ❤

Just look at my life! Should I be feeling gratitude, or have I been ripped off? Is the glass half-empty or half-full?

I can complain that rose bushes have thorns, or I can be grateful that some thorn bushes have roses. At the purely intellectual or "scientific" level, these two attitudes are equivalent. But in real life, it makes a huge difference which we choose.

When the image we hold of ourselves in relationship to the world portrays us as a victim, the resulting sense of helplessness is transmitted through the entire system. The physical consequence of this can be failure or breakdown in an organ or organ system.

Whether we feel gratitude and fullness, or loss, deprivation, and resentment, a corresponding internal chemical state is created. This state, in turn, generates characteristic behaviors—health or disease, empowerment/powerlessness, fulfillment/dissatisfaction, success/failure.

In my medical practice (mind/body medicine), the importance of gratitude is strikingly clear in a psychophysiological way—grateful people heal faster; they are able to eliminate harmful behaviors from their lives with greater ease; they are *happier.*

In twentysomething years of practice, I have made an interesting discovery. There are those who take what they learn from me and make profound changes in their lives; there are others whose symptoms and diseases are exactly the same, who have difficulty healing or changing their behaviors. Patients who are *grateful* for the sessions we have, who appreciate the energy and focus I give to them, are the ones who do well. Those who are suspicious and mistrusting, who think the sessions should be longer or less expensive, who wonder whether they are being "ripped off," are much slower to change. It is obvious from the sequence of events that the gratitude (or lack of it) comes *first*.

The way in which we see the world shapes our responses to the challenges life presents us. A sense of gratitude empowers us to choose wisely...how we feel, what we say, what we believe, what we do. How preposterous for us, who are richer and consume 10 times the resources than 95 percent of the world's people, who routinely live 25 years longer than our greatgrandparents, who bask in personal freedom and potential, to focus on the "half-empty." Gratitude leads us to see what is available, what can develop. After all, there is nothing to work with in the empty part of the glass.

Without the attitude of gratitude, there results a feeling of deprivation well known, for instance, to America's overweight 60 percent. In a similar way, smokers, drinkers, and drug abusers— whose quality of life continuously deteriorates—

are unable to enact the apparently simple choices that they say and truly *believe* they want to make. Such people are in an involuntary state of denial—a denial of the richness that is within them. Consciousness of the fullness of Self would make their compulsions pale by comparison. Without the sense of who you really are, it is difficult to discern the true worth of anything that takes place in your life except at the immediate and transitory level of instant gratification.

Vicious Circle, Virtuous Circle

When we feel grateful, we interact with other people from our fullness; they feel appreciated and are attracted by our energy. Resentment, bitterness, and victimhood tends to repel people, and we experience less support from others. Similarly, when our lack of gratitude leads to helplessness and disease, we feel "ripped off" that our health is going downhill while others are out enjoying themselves.

Learned Gratitude

In the field of psychoneuroimmunology, we are now certain that emotions, beliefs, and interpretations (our map of the world) have a profound effect upon the body's functioning, including whether we become ill or resist disease. Most dramatic are the studies on "learned helplessness." No matter what the challenges or crises in our life may be, if we feel *helpless* about them, we are much more likely to become ill.

The state of mind that we call gratitude is not inborn, in my opinion, but something we learn. Gratitude has to do with feeling full, complete, adequate—we have everything we need and deserve; we approach the world with a sense of value. It is the experience of the range of fulfillment that is possible that leads to a capacity for gratitude. Without gratitude, the tendency is to feel incomplete, cheated, deficient—in a word, *helpless*.

If you were not fortunate enough to have been taught the attitude of gratitude as a child, you may, from time to time, feel yourself slipping into despair, feeling resentful and unblessed. That still happens to me sometimes and, when it does, I simply remember my reasons for doing the things I do, my personal life mission and vision, with gratitude. It may take a little while, but with inner focus and imagery, my attitude always comes around. After all, just like you, "I am what I think."

Transcendental Gratitude

Dan Millman

Dan Millman is the author of seven books, including WAY OF THE PEACEFUL WARRIOR, NO ORDINARY MOMENTS, THE LIFE YOU WERE BORN TO LIVE, and two children's books. His writings (translated into 16 languages) have inspired millions of people. A former world-champion athlete and college professor, Dan now trains people from all walks of life in areas of personal and spiritual growth.

❤   ❤   ❤

Although most of us have five senses, two additional ones have special significance: a sense of humor and a sense of perspective. Out of these grows a natural outpouring of gratitude. If we lack perspective, we also lack humor; we may become upset about small disappointments, broken expectations—about the imperfections or mistakes of others.

However, those of us who have encountered strong challenges and tests, such as pain, illness, and the death of a loved one, have a different reference point. We don't "sweat the small stuff"; we feel thankful for even small favors and blessings. Charles Grodin, the writer and actor, once shared with me that after his father died when Charles was 18 years old, everything else was "small stuff." His father's death gave him a sense of perspective and, with it, a profound sense of gratitude.

Over time, with an expanded perspective, our perceptions change. We begin to feel grateful, not only for particular favors, acts of kindness, or pleasant circumstances, but for small things—the glimpse of a sunrise, the beauty of a tree blowing in a breeze. Perspective also leads to a profound kind of humility, not in the sense of meekness, but in appreciating our place in the larger universe and the opportunity that life represents, whether or not it happens to be going well at the moment.

As children, we were taught conventional gratitude: "Say thank you to Aunt Susan for the nice underwear, dear." Or we might have been "taught" gratitude out of guilt: "Just remember how we've sacrificed for you, and look how you act!" When someone calls us "ungrateful," we've broken one of their social conventions. Conventional gratitude may carry the subtle burden of obligation, bartering favors or keeping score, as if saying, "You've done more for me than I do for you, so I'm in the red, gratitude-wise: I owe you one." Usually a mixture of motives underlies altruistic acts—a sense of duty, obligation, social conscience, a need for recognition, attention, and only rarely, pure altruism or self-sacrifice.

If someone does a favor for me, social convention tells me that I "should" be grateful. But if I've allowed them the opportunity to give, to serve, and to raise their sense of self-worth, perhaps they should be grateful to me. The deeper we look at it, the more elusive the "rules" of gratitude become.

Transcendental gratitude, however, goes beyond social conventions. Instead of feeling grateful to someone, we feel grateful *for* them—for God or Spirit working through them. We begin to feel grateful for everyone and everything that arises in our lives. This feeling uplifts us, embraces us, and helps us to uplift and embrace others in the ultimate recognition that we are, ultimately, in this together.

For some time now, I've been waking up grateful each morning, and I go to sleep grateful each night with a tacit and growing sense of the presence, love, and blessing of Spirit. I feel grateful for my friends and adversaries, for both the joys and challenges of my life, because the joys give me pleasure, and the challenges help me grow. Everything serves in its way.

Falling into Gratitude

Mary-Margaret Moore

Mary-Margaret Moore has been the channel for the Bartholomew energy for the past 17 years. She spent her first 18 years growing up in Hawaii and the next five obtaining two degrees from Stanford University. She has been a seeker of clear awareness for many years, using techniques ranging from the study of the power of Christian saints to Zen Buddhism to the insights of Ramana Maharshi.

One of the things that I have learned in these last 17 years working with the Bartholomew

Awareness is that gratitude, like love, can be experienced at ever-deepening levels. There was a time when I felt that being grateful just meant feeling good about the things in one's life, the people in one's life, and the pleasure in one's life. But Bartholomew has shown us something far vaster than this limited, linear "what's in it for me" point of view. What he has shown repeatedly is that gratitude, at its deepest level, is an ever-present, abundantly peace-filled energy field that is constantly available in every moment of our life, regardless of the circumstances manifesting in that moment. He has turned us away from the identification of "feeling good if things are going well," to the deep and heartfelt reality that this gratitude, this wonder, this peace, is a constant electromagnetic tone that is accessible by just dropping out of our mental and emotional drama and into the silent constancy of gratitude itself.

It is an exciting moment when we realize that whatever comes to us, whatever is present now, is precisely what we need for our awakening to the Vast Infinite Light of Being Itself—God, Love, Light, What Is, Our True Nature—whatever you choose to call it. Bartholomew's constant words to us are, "Whatever is present is It. Whatever you are experiencing, if you will simply allow it to be fully felt and experienced without thinking about it, trying to change it, trying to understand or avoid it, you will find at the core of all experiences the peace and the wonder that you have been seeking."

In these last years, many of us, on all spiritual paths, have begun to truly awaken to this ever-present reality. As I travel the globe, I find that this is true in all countries I visit, with people from so many different backgrounds.

It is as if there is a wellspring of hope and gratitude and insightful awakening happening to thousands upon thousands of seekers from all paths, named and unnamed. What I have heard again and again is people voicing their gratitude that they finally know that God exists; that somehow, by who knows what grace, we are beginning to truly Real-ize that we, as our birthright, have the potential to truly experience the God-ness of our Being. And that this is the potential for this moment, this day, in this life—not in some future, more auspicious rebirth when cir-cumstances are more favorable. We all seem to be willing to finally hear the "good news"—that we are That which we seek, we have never been separate from Who We Are, and that this Reality is ours whenever we are willing to drop out of our mental and emotional temporary creations and into the Eternally Present Presence.

The final letting-go comes when we allow our-selves to Real-ize that each moment can be filled with this warmth when we allow things to be exactly as they are. We can't "do it," "find it," or "earn it." But we can Be It. Because we already are It. What could be easier than Being what we really are? We need to just stop the trying, and what is left is the Vastness of Being. No struggle, no striving—just Being.

My Own "Gratitude Book"

Rev. Nancy Norman

Rev. Nancy Norman is dedicated to inspiring people to discover, develop, and achieve their highest potential. Her approach is clear, practical, sincere, and easily transferable to everyday life. Nancy is a Unity minister and has enjoyed successful careers in real estate, fashion, and education. She devotes her life to helping people live better, fuller, more abundant lives.

The little dark cloud seemed to hover above me at all times, ready to pour down its doom and gloom. Recently divorced, unsure of my future, no job or career in sight, financially insecure and feeling very alone, the little dark cloud never left my side. What was I to do? I didn't even know where to start. Then an idea came to mind. It was as if someone was telling me, "Stop focusing on what isn't right about your life, and begin seeing what is good and positive." Not an original idea, I admit, but one that had not occurred to me before.

A plan began to formulate. I sat down and started to list every good and positive thing I could think of, going back as far as I could remember. As I wrote, the world began to seem friendlier, and I realized how much I had to be grateful for. By the end of the writing session, I had filled pages, and the feelings of doom and gloom were ebbing away. I decided at that point to carry this idea of gratitude—of focusing on what was good and right in my life—a step further. My plan was to carry a small notebook with me at all times and list the things I was grateful for as they occurred.

I took my morning walk and saw the world with new eyes. The scenery that I had taken for granted on other mornings was alive with beauty and color. The dogs I passed, the birds I heard, were all reminders that I lived in an abundant, loving, harmonious Universe. I recorded all these wonders in my "Gratitude Book."

As the day progressed, blessing after blessing occurred. The mail arrived—rather than bills, there were three checks. Unexpected income. A neighbor brought me a wonderful homemade pie; she said that she didn't know why, but she thought of me as she was baking. A friend gave me a painting he had commissioned for me done by a well-known artist. I continued to write these events in my Gratitude Book, and by early afternoon, that little dark cloud of doom and gloom had disintegrated.

I continue to use my Gratitude Book. It helps me see beyond my self-defeating fears and doubts. Gratitude is a powerful magnetic force that naturally draws joyous people and events to me. It attracts the hidden potential in life. Gratitude is one of the greatest secrets of a fulfilled life—it is cooperating with the Universe.

Yes! I do live in a loving, abundant, harmonious Universe, and I am grateful!

The Gift of Gratitude

Robert Odom

Robert Odom, *the author of YOUR COMPANION TO 12 STEP RECOVERY, is a metaphysical counselor, lecturer, and teacher with over 15 years in recovery. He is a student of New Mexico history and, appropriately, makes his home in both Santa Fe, and Las Cruces, New Mexico.*

Learning how to love is a process that involves remembering who we really are. The bottom-line reality is that all life on the planet is a manifestation of Spirit in physical bodies. All life is Spirit, and Spirit is sacred; therefore, all life is sacred.

Gratitude involves taking time to consciously appreciate the complexity of life. Often we can get so busy "doing" that there is little time left for living. Sometimes we can only be grateful for obvious blessings while we wind up resenting our pain.

We live in a culture that programs us to expect instant gratification and to devalue processes that involve large amounts of time and close attention. It is easy for us to read a few books, go to several workshops, and expect immediate enlightenment. It is a mentality of "microwave spirituality." In learning how to love, we must embrace all of life's experiences, both the horrible and the sublime. So often, our greatest spiritual knowing comes cloaked in confusion and pain. It is truly a challenge to become grateful for our pain as well as our joy.

Being grateful for our lessons and for our experiences is actually a way of responding to life, flowing from a full heart. Being grateful, or as we say in 12 Step programs, adopting an "attitude of gratitude," keeps us in touch with our interconnectedness. It reminds us that we are all part of the great spiral of creation, on a spiritual journey back to the Source. Everything on that journey is a part of bringing us closer to Spirit by making us aware of our own divinity.

We have a spiritual responsibility to be consciously grateful because that energy's frequency flows from us and assists in our own healing, our brother's and sister's healing, and ultimately the healing of the planet, our EarthMother.

Take some time to be alone out in nature. Quietly watch the ants, the birds, the leaves in the bushes and trees. All the life forms are unselfconscious in their enjoyment of the world. The ants have more than enough sand to build their hills; the birds have an abundance of twigs for nests; there is far more than enough sunlight for the leaves to produce food for the plants. While you are out there in nature, remember that you, too, are a part of this wonderful, intricate web of life. It is such a glorious blessing to be alive in this wonderful place. Take a deep breath, open your heart, and remember that gratitude is God appreciating the gift of Itself to the world.

Be consciously grateful for every person, place, and thing that helps you learn to love.

Gratitude:
The Natural Expression
of a Loving Heart

❤ ❤ ❤

Daniel T. Peralta

Daniel T. Peralta is a metaphysical teacher with a degree in the Psychology of Consciousness from Antioch University. He has trained extensively with Louise L. Hay. Daniel's work reaches a diverse group of people ranging from children in our public schools to the mentally and emotionally challenged. He is currently working with incarcerated individuals in the prison system. Daniel has also hosted a live interactive television series entitled "Self-Esteem: Becoming Empowered!" on the Education Channel. He resides in Hawaii.

❤ 199

♥   ♥   ♥

Gratitude focuses our attention on
the good things in life.
It takes our blessings and multiplies them.
When we joyfully express appreciation,
it opens our hearts and allows us to
experience more love.

Love is the power that heals our lives, and love is the power that will ultimately heal this world. Gratitude comes from love. It is the natural expression of a loving heart. Therefore, whenever we express gratitude, we align ourselves with the power that heals us. Giving thanks and praise spreads healing energy and makes our lives and the world a better place to be and live. Every time we express appreciation, we help heal the world. Gratitude projects positive vibrations out into the atmosphere, and our benevolent Universe responds kindly.

Therefore, cultivating an "Attitude of Gratitude" is essential. And it begins by noticing all the good that you already have. Counting your blessings is one of the surest ways to lift your spirits. It always shifts the energy to something positive and desirable. If you're feeling depressed or sad, you can start thinking about all the good things in your life. Begin by being grateful for all the blessings you have. Look for them; they're there. This will change your energy. Say thank you to Life for the good that is already abundantly present within you and around you.

The fact that you are alive and are experiencing the gift of life is a tremendous honor. Each new day is alive with new possibilities that you can experience. Each new day is another opportunity for you to begin again. You get another chance at being the wonderful person you are. What a blessing! Thank God that you are here, willing and able to contribute your talents and gifts to this world. The world needs you, and Life is grateful for you. Now it's time to be grateful for yourself.

When you express gratitude, you raise the vibrations around you to a higher frequency. You create positive energy that emanates out from you and returns to you as wonderful experiences. You become magnetic. Good things and good people gravitate toward you because you are such a joy and delight to be around. An attitude of gratitude is naturally attractive. It has the power to turn challenges into possibilities, problems into solutions, and losses into gains. It shifts the energy. It expands our vision and allows us to see what might normally be invisible to someone with a limiting attitude.

Even in our darkest hours, we can cultivate an attitude of gratitude. No matter what is happening around us, we can choose to respond in a way that will help us learn and grow. When we look at our difficulties as opportunities for growth, then we can be grateful for the lessons we are learning from these difficult experiences. There is always a gift in every experience. Expressing gratitude allows us to find it. When we are genuinely appreciative for all that Life has to offer, we see the Light in ourselves and everyone else. We see everyone and everything as a potential blessing.

Gratitude is a prayer for goodness to abound. It attracts abundance and generosity. I think the words *thank you* are two of the most beautiful words in the language. They can light up someone's face and help the other person know that he or she is appreciated. It opens the door to our hearts and allows us to feel connected.

Every morning upon waking up, the first words out of my mouth are "Thank you." This allows me to feel immediately connected with God and fills my heart with love. I am grateful that I am alive and breathing and have another day to live life fully and richly. I am thankful that I am here, participating and partaking in the lavish abundance of this Universe.

Life's bounty is here for all of us. When we express love and gratitude, we harmonize our energies and awaken to the knowing that our very own lives are part of this rich bounty.

Here are some tips for cultivating an attitude of gratitude:

- ❤ *Throughout the day, say the words* thank you *either silently or aloud. Let God know that you are happy to be alive and participating in this experience called Life. Say thank you to yourself, others, and the world. Let the attitude of gratitude spread.*

- ❤ *Keep a gratitude book. Write down all the things you are grateful for in your life. Remember to include things such as electricity, water, plumbing, technology, and all those modern conveniences we often overlook. If you can't physically write them down, then do it mentally. Praise the progress we have all made.*

❤ *When you're having hard times, look at the experiences and say, "I know that this has come to bless me, and I am willing to see the gift in this experience. May the lessons be revealed to me, and may I become stronger and clearer."*

Thank you....Thank you...Thank you...
Thank you...

Gratitude: A Lifestyle

Marcia Perkins-Reed

Marcia Perkins-Reed is a nationally known motivational speaker and seminar presenter. She brings to her audiences a combination of 25 years of varied business experience, degrees in psychology and law, ten years in New Thought, and the success and fulfillment experienced by her and her consulting clients. Marcia is the author of the book WHEN 9 TO 5 ISN'T ENOUGH: A GUIDE TO FINDING FULFILLMENT AT WORK.

Gratitude isn't always easy to invoke. If our circumstances are unpleasant, or if we are concentrating more on what we lack than on what we have, it may seem ludicrous to try to find something to be thankful for. But gratitude comprises more than simply being thankful. Thankfulness is directed toward a specific object or event that has just happened, as in "I am thankful for the new sweater I just received." Gratitude, by contrast, is a lifestyle—a way of living. People who live in a state of gratitude have developed the ability to embody, moment by moment, a sense of wonder and contentment with their lives just as they are. And as they do so, they paradoxically seem to attract more and more blessings into their lives in the form of money, fulfilling jobs, deeply satisfying personal relationships, and other things that they desire.

Expressing thankfulness on a regular basis can lead to a gratitude-filled lifestyle. I have developed a practice, every time something good happens—whether expected or not!—to say (to myself or out loud): "Thank you, God!" But as you do this regularly, you will begin to notice yourself changing. Things that used to bother you don't bother you as much anymore. You see someone less fortunate than yourself, and as you thank your Source for what you have, you also reach out to help the other person and to give him or her what you can of yourself and your substance.

Practicing gratitude is simply recognizing that there is infinite substance all around us, throughout the universe and beyond. And we must, as Eric Butterworth urges us in his book *Spiritual Economics,* "Get it into your consciousness that you live in substance as a fish lives in water." We can never lack substance, even if we lose all of our assets in a financial crisis—for substance is the nonmaterial essence of the things we see. So we can always invoke gratitude for the invisible substance around us, knowing that as we do so, we will draw its manifestation to us.

Gratitude leads to two delightful results in our lives. First, it creates a deep sense of joy. It is said that if we pursue happiness as our goal, it will elude us. The same is true of joy: If we seek it for its own sake, we will not find it. But if we practice gratitude—living in a consciousness of contentment, being thankful for what we have (even if it is meager), and cultivating inner peace through times of quiet meditation—we will find that joy appears spontaneously.

The second result of gratitude is a personal experience of abundance and prosperity. It is an accepted principle that "what we focus on expands." If we spend most of our time thinking about what we don't have, or how we wish our life was different, or what we just lost, that will expand—and we will have more loss, more lack, and more discontent with our current situation. If, on the other hand, we focus on what we have—food on the table, friends and/or family who care about us, the sunshine outside—that, too, will expand. The energy of gratitude in our lives draws more and more of the things we desire to us, almost by magic.

So begin your practice of gratitude today. As you awaken, immediately ask yourself, "What can I be thankful for today?" Spend time in the silence of your own inner self, appreciating the wonder of who you are. And remember to always acknowledge the good that comes to you.

Gratitude:
A Powerful Force

John Randolph Price

John Randolph Price *is the author of numerous bestselling books, including THE SUPERBEINGS, THE ABUNDANCE BOOK, THE ANGELS WITHIN US, and PRACTICAL SPIRITUALITY. He is the board chairman of The Quartus Foundation, and with his wife Jan, he conducts workshops and intensive gatherings. In recognition of their work in initiating the Global Mind-Link and World Healing Day, the Prices were named the 1986 recipients of the "Light of God Expressing Award" by the Association of Unity Churches. John was also given the 1992 Humanitarian*

Award by the Arizona District of the International New Thought Alliance.

❤   ❤   ❤

The common meaning of gratitude is to be thankful for benefits received. While this is important, I feel that the energy of gratitude is one of the most powerful *attracting* forces in the universe. A heart filled with thanksgiving, even when appearances tell us that we are mired in scarcity, conflict, and affliction, moves us to a higher frequency in consciousness—and we soon witness reality shining through the illusion.

To paraphrase what I've written in my book *Empowerment,* our desires are first fulfilled in consciousness, and then they come forth in the outer world as the ideal experience and form—so the secret is to be thankful while our good is still invisible. Gratitude releases a dynamic current of spiritual energy to go before us to exert a mighty influence in our world. It not only eliminates negative patterns in the subconscious caused by ingratitude, it also forms a connecting link—a bridge—to every possible source of good. Of course, there is only one Source, but Divine Mind works in mysterious ways to perform magnificent wonders through an infinite number of channels. And through a feeling of gratitude, we put ourselves in alignment with universal riches, loving relations, and the healing power of Spirit radiating from within.

My wife Jan and I have proved the power of gratitude many times in our lives. In the 1970s, I was having a difficult time in a business situation and had spent days praying and meditating for a solution. Then one morning as I was getting out of bed, I heard an audible voice boom through our bedroom with the words *"Quiet trust."* To me, that meant that the problem had been solved, and my role in the scheme of things was to still my mind (that is, stop worrying) and trust the divine process. A feeling of intense gratitude came over me, and for the next several days, my constant expression in mind and heart was *Thank you, God!* And then suddenly out of chaos came perfect order and harmony.

On December 30, 1993, when Jan had a heart attack and died on the EMS gurney in our home, I felt a sense of detachment and little emotional response. Even when the paramedic said to me, "I'm sorry, we've lost her," I wouldn't accept it. On some level of consciousness, I knew she would come back and would recover quickly. After more than four minutes on the other side, she did return, and later at the hospital while waiting for a report from the doctors, I let that feeling of gratitude rise up as never before. My prayer in the waiting room was one of great thankfulness for the Lifeforce within her that was healing and perfecting her body. The next morning, Jan, too, was expressing gratitude for life, her incredible experience, and how wonderful she felt—and the doctor was shaking his head in thankful awe of her rapid recovery. Gratitude, which combines the energies of love and joy, had filled that hospital to overflowing, and it would not have surprised me to learn that other miraculous healings had taken place during that time.

When we live with grateful hearts, fear cannot enter, guilt is dissolved, and there is only peace, love, forgiveness, and understanding. To me, that's what life is all about.

A Shortcut to a Miracle

Rev. Michael C. Rann

Rev. Michael C. Rann is the minister of the First Church of Religious Science in Chicago, and the author of several books, including EFFECTIVE RADIO ADVERTISING, SOMETHING GOOD IS ABOUT TO HAPPEN, and THE POWER OF COMMITMENT. Michael is a charismatic and dynamic speaker whose philosophy of life is one of success for himself, for his clients, and for all those with whom he comes in contact.

If there is a shortcut to manifesting a miracle, it is though an *attitude of gratitude*. When individuals learn to be thankful, they are opening their lives to receptive action. Thankfulness evokes the *Law of Receptivity*.

Learning to use two simple words, *thank you,* helps you accomplish things you desire. For example, if you would like a particular table in a restaurant, thank the host or hostess in advance; it usually gets you a seat at a table positioned exactly where you want to be seated. I could go on with more examples, but I'm sure you understand the point that I am making.

Did you ever think of what happens when you say thank you when you are grateful? Let's think about it for a moment. You say thank you, and in a split second, there is a closeness established between you and the person you thanked. For the person you say it to, it makes him or her feel wanted, appreciated, and even important. In other words, saying thank you makes the person feel good.

The simple fact is that you cannot give without receiving. This, all the learned philosophers tell us, is a Law. "We give what we choose, and we receive back that which we give. So, in fact, we choose what we receive in life." How sad for those who have not learned this simple truth.

Don't take my word or anyone else's word for it. Try it yourself! Say thank you, and watch the results in your life. Then try saying thank you even before the desired results occur. You will be amazed by how quickly your life becomes filled with wonderful outcomes that some choose to call *miracles*.

What does saying thank you do for you? When you make another person feel good, you also feel good. When you make another person feel important, you also feel important. How wonderful it is to help yourself feel good, important, and even appreciated. Saying thank you to others gives you the same respect and satisfaction that you expressed to the one whom you thanked.

Following this way of life is a wonderful adventure. To know any Law is to respect it, and the *Laws of Gratitude and Receptivity* are an established science. To have faith in these Laws and to practice them on a regular basis allows the Creative Power to work for you.

The possibilities are awesome when you learn to appreciate and respect the things that others do to make your life more enjoyable. You create your own experience, so let it be one filled with respect and appreciation. Since it is up to you to choose what your experience will be, you have an opportunity to demonstrate this form of love, and love *always* produces constructive, creative action.

It all starts with an *attitude of gratitude* and with saying the two simple words, *thank you*. You cannot give good away. It keeps coming back bigger and better than when you gave it. Now it's up to you! Prove the power of gratitude, and you will be practicing what some refer to as the highest form of prayer.

Oh, by the way, thank you for reading this essay. I appreciate your time, and I appreciate YOU!

Gratitude:
Its Healing Properties

Dr. Frank Richelieu

Dr. Frank Richelieu *is pastor of the Church of Religious Science of Redondo Beach, California, and a past president of Religious Science International. He received much of his religious training from Ernest Holmes, the founder of the Religious Science movement. Dr. Richelieu's dynamic talks are heard over radio daily on the "Living Ideas" program, which has been broadcast for 25 years. He is the author of THE PROSPERITY CONNECTION, REINCARNATION: THE INHERITANCE OF A SOUL, and THE ART OF BEING YOURSELF.*

♥ ♥ ♥

Gratitude is more than an ennobling attitude. It is one of the most empowering, healing, dynamic instruments of consciousness vital to demonstrating the life experiences one desires. When you are focused on gratitude, you are filled with the awareness of the good and desirable fabric of your life. You are literally praising and blessing what you know you already have. This knowing is the fulfilling of a cosmic law: WHAT YOU ADORE BECOMES MORE.

Gratitude is like a magnet. It draws and attracts to you that which is equal to it. If, for example, you happen to be flat on your back in pain, practice gratitude in the area of health. Be grateful for the health you do have. Focus on the feeling of peace and well-being that still exists in other parts of your body. When experiencing illness of any kind, it is especially essential to let your mind dwell on health with gratitude and acceptance for the good. See that the greater part of your body is doing what you want it to. Praise and bless it. Your body is renewable and rechargeable. Your gratitude is like fertilizer to the tree of your life. It stimulates health and growth.

When you are seemingly overwhelmed by a chaotic condition or situation, that is the time to think of the peace at the heart of the infinite. That is the time to flood your mind and emotions with peace in grateful thanks for the Divine Law and Order that exists throughout the universe, making Law and Order a possibility for you, as well. As you become filled with gratitude for health and peace, the solutions and the healing fall right into place. When you do not know how you are going to meet next month's financial obligations and you become filled with tension and the idea of lack, realize that the divine antidote is to be thankful for abundance. When in the midst of any problem or situation, say to yourself:

> *I am thankful for perfect health and abun-*
> *dant good that finds its way to me by*

means of the avenues in my life that I have made open and available for the divine flow. I am thankful for all the joy that arises in my consciousness. I am thankful for the abundant health that is mine now. I am grateful for the opportunity to know more and grow more in consciousness.

What you give your attention to is what you manifest in your life. The teacher Jesus knew this to such an extent that he could give thanks for that which was not visible, knowing that it would become tangible and factual by means of the Law of Cause and Effect. What we call problems are very close to us. They trap us on every level— physically, mentally, and emotionally. They are so "visible" that it is difficult for us to be objective about them. It is necessary to take our attention from them and place it on the desired result, which is already complete in Infinite Mind.

We must see beyond problems to the answered prayer. We must bring the invisible into the visi-

ble by dwelling on what we want within consciousness instead of dwelling on what appears
to be. This is the way in which we turn problems
into opportunities. This is the way we release the
tension and congestion and move through whatever appears to be creating trouble. As we do so,
we move into the realm of the solution. Many of
us give thanks and are grateful for what we have,
but how many of us give thanks for what we are
about to receive? Try to form a practice of saying:

> *I am thankful for the blessings I am about
> to receive. I am thankful for the increased
> harmonious conditions in my home. I am
> thankful for the wonderful experiences that
> exacerbate my growth. I am thankful for
> the newness that I am about to receive. I
> am thankful that I have an attitude of grat-
> itude about the living of life. My attitude of
> gratitude opens the portals to richer living.*

By doing so, you will not be working on things
and conditions, but on your own consciousness.

You will be programming it to expect the best. You cannot have an attitude of gratitude and also be bitter. You must be free of the idea that people or situations are against you. You must also be free of the belief that you have made a mess of your life and there is nothing you can do about it.

When gratitude rises within you like a fountain, it brings in its wake greater health, greater joy, greater supply, greater prosperity, and greater opportunity for living life than you have ever experienced before. If you seem overwhelmed by a situation or problem and cannot see your way clear to think and feel gratitude, do this:

Sit down and go back in consciousness to the memory of things for which you can be truly grateful. Think how God has guided and directed you through past problems. Once you have a sincere feeling of gratitude for those past blessings, realize that the same God is with you today, guiding, directing, renewing, and restoring. Then project your thoughts beyond the present situation, and be grateful for what you are about to receive.

The Psalms are songs of praise and thanksgiving and were sung during times of trouble. In the midst of dire conditions and situations, the Psalmist's faith never wavered. He praised and blessed and was thankful, for he knew that God was ever present, running the universe and creating ultimate good. Perhaps he did not always understand why such conditions were occurring; the human viewpoint is very limited in times of trouble, but his faith never wavered.

Gratitude is important because it is not just a cold, mental acceptance of something. It is warm like the sunshine that makes the flowers grow. It unfreezes the condition and makes it possible for the desired good to become manifest.

Rejoice in your freedom of choice. You are a law unto yourself. Say to yourself right now:

Gratitude is a healing power that enters into every part of my being, transforming, strengthening, renewing, and making it whole. Gratitude is ever flowing through me now. I am filled with a deep inner feeling of gratitude that enriches my every experience.

Thank You, God

Murray Salem

Murray Salem is an actor and screenwriter who wrote the Arnold Schwarzenegger hit film KINDERGARTEN COP. He resides in Los Angeles with his three cats, Blue, Grey, and Kiri.

My paternal grandmother, long since passed away, was a simple Syrian peasant woman who could neither read nor write. Yet she was devoutly religious. No matter what she was doing, God was always on her lips. But more than just His name, she would say, "Thank you, God; thank you, God" at least a hundred times a day. And *not* just when good things happened. The soup would boil over, making a terrible mess. As she cleaned it up, she would be saying, "Thank you, God. Thank you. Thank you, God."

I asked her why she was thanking God for something bad. She laughed and said because when something bad happens, that's when we forget our connection to God (that is, our Higher Power). At the time, it seemed very bizarre to me, since she insisted that I do it, too. I'd scrape my knee, and she'd tell me to say, "Thank you, God." Oddly enough it seemed to work, and my knee would feel better.

Then I turned five and started school. Since I was from an ethnic background, the blue-eyed, blond-haired kids used to make fun of me. Because of my dark complexion, their nickname for me was "Nigger." I hated school, and I begged my parents not to make me go anymore. They felt bad for me, but they couldn't protect me forever. Then my Situ (Syrian for *grandmother*) heard what was happening and told me that I should say, "Thank you, God" every time the kids called me horrible names. At the time, I thought that was the dumbest suggestion I'd ever heard.

But a few days after she talked to me, when a whole group of boys started shouting, "Nigger! Nigger! Nigger!," something happened. I was holding back the tears, trying with every ounce of strength in my body not to be a "sissy" and let them see me cry. But I couldn't stop myself. The tears were going to burst out anyway.

Then I remembered Situ's "Thank you, God." I started repeating it silently to myself. *Thank you, God. Thank you, God.* It helped! I don't know exactly what happened, but the tears subsided. Suddenly, I didn't care so much what they thought. Maybe that's because I felt that I now had a friend, too—God.

That was all a very long time ago. Since then, I've become a successful screenwriter. I've traveled

the world and met hundreds of wonderful people. My life is more than I ever expected. And
through it all, I've kept on saying, "Thank you,
God." Sometimes I say it a hundred times a day,
just like my dear grandmother. I even feel like
saying it now.

"Thank you, God. Thank you. Thank you, God."

In All Things Give Thanks

Dr. J. Kennedy Shultz

Dr. J. Kennedy Shultz is founder and pastor of the Atlanta Church of Religious Science. He is well known as a teacher and lecturer in the field of New Thought, with his lectures and seminars widely distributed on audiocassettes throughout the United States and abroad. Dr. Shultz holds a master's degree in counseling from New York University, and Religious Science International awarded him recognition as Doctor of Religious Science in 1987 when he was first elected president of that organization. He is the author of A LEGACY OF TRUTH and YOU ARE THE POWER.

❤   ❤   ❤

The great German philosopher Goethe, toward the end of his long life, said that there would be very little left of him if he were to discard all that he owed to others. As I get older, and hopefully wiser, I am certain that this is absolutely true for me, also. Everything substantial about me is made out of the good that people have given me along the way, which I have had the good sense to accept; and the harm people have done me along the way, which I have had the grace to forgive. I learned much from every bit of it once I became grateful for the power in me that lets me own the experience beyond the event.

This means that we need to be grateful that we have received some enduring good from the wonderful things people have given us or done for us and from whatever harm done unto us that we have survived. You don't survive real harm without a growth in wisdom. And sometimes, it seems, we require that our wisdom comes to us the hard way through survival of the worst.

It is not possible to take our wisdom back in time and do it all over again the right way. It is only possible to take wisdom, however it comes, and go forward with it, doing things better than we did before. But no good thing belongs to us until we own it. And we do not own anything that we do not accept with gratitude. In other words, it's not yours until you say thank you. Thank who? Thank God! It is not always easy to thank people for what we have gotten out of our relationship with them. But it is always possible to thank God that we have come out of it with something of value. And once you get used to thanking God for all life on a regular basis, it becomes clear who else you ought to be thanking, and it becomes easy to do so.

When we subscribe to the old admonition to "in all things give thanks," we are not agreeing to give thanks *for* all things. It is not sensible to be thankful for bad things, harmful things. Rather than be carried mindlessly away with the good things or driven into the ground by the bad things, take the time in the midst of all things to be grateful to God that you are greater than both the best of them and the worst of them, and that you will find a way to come out of any of them, somehow enhanced by the experience.

An attitude of gratitude in the midst of all things will allow us to make all things new. It will allow us to make something better out of both the best and the worst that comes our way, because an attitude of gratitude puts us in right relationship with God, the creative power of our lives. And our creative power flows forth best into our minds and hearts when we are open to it. So don't clog up the Divine wavelengths of your consciousness by fears that the good that is coming your way won't last forever, or that the bad you are experiencing will. Just take the time in the midst of it all to be thankful that there is an eternally durable wisdom at work within you that knows how to use it all to your ultimate advantage. If you do this, you make yourself a person who moves through life retaining the best and discarding the rest as a matter of course. This takes the struggle out of daily living in this funny old world of ours and sets us free to live more

easily. The more easily we forgive, the more easily we live. And the more naturally grateful we
become for what life really is, the freer we
become of the kind of nonsense that used to trip
us up and demean our existence.

I am quite taken by this quotation from the great
Meister Eckhart: *"Be always ready for the gifts of
God, and always for new ones—and always
remember, God is a thousand times more ready to
give than you are to receive."*

The stuff that blocks our readiness to receive is
all the stuff that clogs up our consciousness when
we do not know how to respond to life with gratitude for our God-given power to make the best
out of both the good and the bad. A sincere and
inspired religious effort to develop a relationship
of perpetual thanksgiving with God will clear out
that fearful stuff and "make ready the way of the
Lord." This is the mind that in all things remem-
bers to give thanks.

The Power of Gratitude

Ron Scolastico, Ph.D.

Ron Scolastico, Ph.D., is a distinguished academic psychologist, spiritual counselor, and author with over 25 years' experience in the study of human consciousness. Since 1978, Ron has been the voice for the profound wisdom of "the Guides," loving spiritual beings who exist beyond physical reality. He is the author of THE EARTH ADVENTURE; HEALING THE HEART, HEALING THE BODY; and DOORWAY TO THE SOUL.

The power of gratitude can often be overlooked in the complexity of day-to-day life. Many people do not know that feelings of gratitude can set into motion potent, beneficial changes within the human personality.

For example, feelings of gratitude can create an emotional softening and a deepening of love in your experience of yourself and your life, bringing about greater joy and happiness in your human expression. Gratitude can also stimulate strong inner energies within you that can lead to a blossoming of your intuitive abilities, enabling you to eventually have a deeper spiritual experience and to become more aware of your existence as an eternal soul.

To gain a clear understanding of gratitude, you can look at such feelings in relation to two general areas of life. The first area is gratitude for *permanent* aspects of your existence, which include the spiritual realities of life that interact with your human expression. The second area is gratitude for *temporary,* transitory experiences in the physical world.

To be grateful for permanent aspects of your life, you can begin to pay attention to your ability to experience yourself as one individual living within a physical body. You have the extraordinary capacity to be aware of your Self—to feel, "I am me." You have the capacity to think, to feel, and to act in the physical world. These aspects of your existence are often taken for granted. If you can become aware of the incredible complexity of energies that have been wielded by eternal souls to make it possible for you to live in your physical body in this moment, you will be filled with an overwhelming feeling of gratitude and love for your body, for your Self, for other human beings, and for all of life.

Your permanent magnificence is also tied to beautiful, powerful, spiritual energies that constantly flow into you from the forces that have created life. You are not usually aware of these divine forces of creativity, but if you set aside a few moments of silence each day to attune to them, you can learn to *feel* them. Such experiences can stimulate a great awakening within you. You can fully appreciate and celebrate the constantly occurring miracles in the spiritual dimensions that enable you to continue to live a human life in the physical world. Through such experiences, you will find it easy to awaken the power of gratitude within your personality.

The second area of gratitude is related to your human expression, which is rooted in desire, ambition, fulfillment, pleasure, displeasure, and other important aspects of your subjective experience. If, on a certain day, you have negative experiences, such as a loss of money or a disappointment in love, then you are not likely to feel much gratitude. If, on another day, you are given millions of dollars as a prize, it will be very easy to feel grateful. Thus, you will usually feel gratitude when you have pleasing experiences and your desires are fulfilled, and you will find it difficult to be grateful when your subjective experiences are negative. These are quite "natural" responses in which the affairs of the human world tend to *dictate* when you will feel grateful.

What is important here is to encourage as many experiences of gratitude as you can, no matter what is happening in your day-to-day life, so that you are not manipulated by circumstances and by your feelings about them. In other words, if you only feel grateful for your life when everything goes well, then during periods of challenge you will be devoid of the important feelings of gratitude.

You can learn to take a few moments in each day to feel grateful for life, even when you are feeling challenged. You can say to yourself:

No matter what I might be feeling about the events in my life in this moment, I do not need to be manipulated by my feelings. I have the freedom to release my normal thoughts and feelings, open my heart to the magnificence of my soul, and of God itself, and begin to feel deeply grateful for the opportunity to be alive in human form in this moment.

It is also of great benefit for you to try to extend the range of things that you are willing to be grateful for, beyond experiences that please you. You can be grateful for experiences that help others, even when they require effort on your part. You can be grateful for growth, even when they require effort on your part. You can be grateful for growth, even when it is brought about by challenging circumstances. At times, challenging life situations can stimulate you more than pleasurable experiences to express greater courage, strength, commitment, and creativity. You can be grateful that challenging situations bring you closer to other human beings, encouraging you to more fully express your capacity for empathy and compassion.

By extending your range of appreciation to more and more life situations, you can feel grateful for your life, even when your own desires are not being fulfilled. Learning to create strong feelings of gratitude during many different life situations can help you feel more powerful, more creative, and more fulfilled.

In each day, whether your momentary human experience is joyful or challenging, you can stimulate more of the power of gratitude by saying to yourself:

I rejoice that I have the extraordinary opportunity to live the miracle of human existence on the physical earth. I am grateful for the variety of experiences that are available to me in my human life. And I celebrate the loving forces of my soul, and of God, that make my life possible.

Gratitude:
A State of Mind

Bernie S. Siegel, M.D.

Bernie S. Siegel, M.D., *is a retired general/pedi-atric surgeon who is now involved in humaniz-ing medical care and medical education. He is the founder of EcaP (Exceptional Cancer Patients) and is the author of LOVE, MEDICINE & MIRACLES; and PEACE, LOVE & HEALING.*

I believe that gratitude is a state of mind, rather than a condition of life related to health or wealth. Let me say that some of my greatest gratitude teachers are the people I call the prisoners of life. What do I mean by that? I mean the people who are imprisoned in bodies or institutions and yet are grateful for life. I believe that once you are grateful for life, seeing it as an opportunity to give love, your life is changed and lived as it was meant to be lived by our Creator.

Examples of this are people I know with a variety of diseases and handicaps whom I call healthy. Why are they healthy? They have learned what my associate's father (a general practitioner) once said: "True good health is the ability to live without it."

Sam Keen tells of a friend of his with Lou Gehrig's disease. He is severely ill, and even breathing is a problem. Sam was visiting him, and he complimented his friend on his attitude. The friend asked, "What choice do I have?" and Sam said, "You could piss and moan a little." His friend said, "It never occurred to me." Yet most people, if you ask them if life is fair, will shout

NO at you. The richer they are, the louder they shout. What we have to realize is that while life is difficult, it is not unfair. We all have our problems. The key is to learn how to live with them and even how to use them.

My mother's message to me was, "It was meant to be. God is redirecting you. Something good will come of this." She was much like Carl Jung, whom I am told, would tell those friends who reported a tragic event, "Let us open a bottle of wine. Something good will come of this." If they reported some wonderful event, he would say, "That's too bad, but if we stick together, maybe we can get you through this." You may laugh, but over 90 percent of lottery winners, three to five years after winning, are complaining that it ruined their lives.

What does the Bible or the Talmud tell us? The Bible says that the son of man comes not to be served, but to serve and to ransom his life for the good of the many. The Talmud tells us that he who rejoices in the afflictions that are brought upon the self brings salvation to the world. Other religions also teach us of the gift or lesson that may be found in an affliction or adversity. Even in Job we learn that afflictions heal, and adversity opens you to a new reality.

Over God's desk are Her favorite sayings that will help you to lighten your burden and feel grateful for life as an opportunity to give love in your unique way. The first one says, "Don't feel totally, personally, irrevocably, eternally responsible for everything. That's my job." And it's signed "God." The other says, "Everything you remember I forget, and everything you forget, I remember."

So here we are living among all the difficulties and pain, and what is it that really makes us grateful and teaches us what a treasure life is? Our mortality. Yes, without our physical and emotional pain, we would not survive. They protect us and awaken us to care for our needs and the needs of those we love. Our mortality teaches us of our limited time here and heightens our awareness of what a treasure life is. As Peter Noll shared in his final journal, "Time isn't money. Time is everything. Seeing something for the last time is almost as good as seeing it for the first time, and you spend more time with the things and people you love and less with the things and people you don't love."

I can only share with you that I am grateful for life and the chance to share in all the wonder of creation, at the same time feeling and knowing much pain. Most of all, I am simply grateful to awaken in the morning and be aware of the world around me. I know that there are others who would choose not to awaken the next morning, and why do we differ?

I think that underlying the difference is the love I have received from the moment of my birth, and that makes it easier for me to feel grateful. I ask all of you, please treat each other the way a loving mother would, so we can all be grateful for life. How you love I leave up to you. Just choose your way of serving out of love, and whenever you meet people, please express that love.

If we do this, then every child will be grateful for life and the opportunity to serve and make a difference in the lives of others. Despite all this, remember that gratitude is always a choice and must come out of free will. The Garden of Eden didn't last because there were no choices. We have a choice. Let us love life, our fellow living things, and be grateful.

Looking Through the Eyes of Gratitude

Rev. Christian Sorenson

*Rev. **Christian Sorenson** is the senior minister at Seaside Church of Religious Science in Del Mar, California. He is past president of the clergy in Southern California and has served on the International Board of Trustees for the Religious Science Movement. As a world traveler and seeker of Truth, he has guided hundreds on spiritual explorations through China, India, Africa, and other exotic lands. As a lifelong student of metaphysics, Christian's intention is to see Spirit in all things.*

❤   ❤   ❤

For the holidays, in my fifth year of life, my grandmother gave me a bow tie that said "Happy New Year" across the front. It was not my favorite gift. In fact, I prayed that I would never have to wear it. But the thank-you letter I had to write is my earliest memory of gratitude. As I wrote that letter, I connected in mind, as we do in any letter writing, with my grandmother, who represented all love and all caring to me. And I also experienced a sense of appreciation for even the least of my holiday booty.

Such early lessons in gratitude instilled in me a lifelong habit of extending thanks that has paid rich dividends in my world. When we see the good, we can't help but focus on the affirmative, which naturally frees us from the heavy negatives that seem to dominate some people's thinking. As I talk with successful people, I hear individuals who are focused on opportunity and possibility, not risk and difficulty. These are people who are grateful for their success thus far and are expecting life to treat them well. And so it does.

Ernest Holmes, the founder of Religious Science, writes in his book *Science of Mind*: "Within us is the unborn possibility of limitless experience. Ours is the privilege of giving birth to it!" Life is waiting for you to trust in its dreams. When we choose to align with the positive flow, then we can be grateful for the difficulties that present themselves and see them as opportunities to bring forth greater good. And, all the while, we are growing and learning in the process.

A grateful heart recharges the soul and revitalizes the body. It releases our soul from bondage, lifts our awareness to a comfortable place where the wings of consciousness can let us soar in harmony with the Creative Intelligence. A wonderful practice to perform first thing in the morning, even before opening your eyes, is to see and feel all the good things in your life. Instead of saying, "Oh, God, it's morning," try "Thank God for this good morning" or "It's another wonderful day. I'm so glad to be alive. This is the day the Lord has made. I will rejoice and be glad in it." Count at least a dozen of your blessings before you get out of bed. You'll be amazed at how much better your day will go. (But beware! Being cheerful before others have had their coffee is not always appreciated!)

Life is an abundant broadcasting system, just waiting for us to tune in to its infinite varieties. As we turn our attention to the positive side through praise and appreciation, we bring ourselves into harmony with this giving frequency. There seems to be a magnetic force that draws our awareness to the ever-present and expanding good. It's as if our conscious and subconscious work diligently to attract only those experiences that support our state of mind. Looking through the eyes of gratitude, we become a channel to bring forth more things to be grateful for. We are told to "be thankful for all things." This includes bow ties, our body, and our daily breath.

It's easy to be grateful for the grand things in life, but to be appreciative for "all things" puts you in a powerful, harmonious place. This morning, as I sat on the bluffs of Del Mar in front of my house, greeting the day, I was immersed in so much beauty that it filled me with a sense of awe. I felt a oneness with the pelicans as they glided inches above the water. I sensed the joy of the dolphins surfing the big waves. And, as I caught a glimpse of the whales lifting their majestic fins above the water, I knew the majesty of God. But this morning, in the rapture of the moment, I also caught a glimpse of myself breathing in unison, it seemed, with the ebb and flow of the tide that appeared to be in perfect rhythm with the wind, the grass rippling in perfect concordance with the rest. And in this moment, I was acutely aware of every grain of sand which, I sensed in the pit of my stomach, was resonating in perfect balance with the whole of the universe.

When I returned to a state of individuality, what else could I say about that experience but... *thank you.*

The Manifestation of Gratitude

Hal Stone, Ph.D., and Sidra Stone, Ph.D.

Hal Stone, Ph.D., and Sidra Stone, Ph.D., both clinical psychologists, are the authors of EMBRACING OUR SELVES, EMBRACING EACH OTHER, and EMBRACING YOUR INNER CRITIC. Hal founded the Center for the Healing Arts in Los Angeles in the early '70s, one of the first holistic health facilities in the country. Sidra directed Hamburger in Los Angeles, a residential treatment center for adolescent girls. Since 1982, they have been traveling and teaching in the U.S. and abroad, in addition to their training and writing activities, which take place at their home on California's north coast in Mendocino County.

❤   ❤   ❤

There is no human emotion, no matter how positive it may appear, that is inherently good or bad. Everything depends on how we use or channel these emotions and feelings. It is our ability to be aware of a particular energy, as well as to make appropriate choices in regard to how this energy manifests in the world, which determines how we use any idea or feeling or experience. It is only in this way that we can judge whether or not a particular emotion or idea is manifesting in a way that is a force for good or evil in the world. Gratitude is no exception to this kind of rule.

Gratitude and love, so often experienced together, are both relational in nature. That is to say, it requires someone to feel the gratitude, and it requires someone or some group of persons to be doing something that produces the gratitude. The issue of gratitude is also very basic in transformational work because it is generally a core feeling found in individuals who are helped by a consciousness teacher of any kind, Used in this way, it is a part of the transference relationship that exists between the student, on the one hand, and the teacher, on the other hand, in any teaching, training, or therapeutic relationship. For the purposes of this essay, the word *teacher* will include any therapeutic modality such as therapist, healer, or writer. *Student* will include any recipient of help, whether it is a client, subject, patient, or seeker.

One of the confusing things about gratitude is that it can be experienced by an individual in a number of different ways. How it is experienced and how it manifests over time has a strong effect on how someone's process goes. We want to focus on how gratitude manifests with and without awareness and what the consequences are of each condition. We also plan to focus on the issue as it specifically applies to the teacher/student relationship in therapy, healing, and small and large group work with individuals who are seeking a greater consciousness.

Without awareness, gratitude tends to manifest through the child side of a person. What we mean by the child side is that there is a parent/child interaction between the teacher and student and that the student is in the role of son or daughter to the teacher. The feelings that occur here can be very strong, but they occur within the parameters of the parent/child interaction. We refer to this parent/child interaction as a bonding pattern.

For example, someone who is helped by a spiritual teacher tends to fall into a particular kind of emotional relationship with the teacher. The student is filled with gratitude and love, and truly his or her cup runneth over. This is a natural, organic part of the teacher/student relationship and the love and gratitude that are a part of spiritual initiation in general. It is not meant, however, to remain in this form forever.

What are the consequences of such a parent/child interaction? How could something so beautiful possibly become something negative? If there is too much gratitude from a child space, empowerment becomes much more difficult to attain because the underlying vulnerability remains unconscious. What happens then is that the Inner Child (vulnerability) of the student is cared for by the teacher. In such a situation, the student may continue to grow on a spiritual level, but there will be fostered a dependency on the teacher and a tendency to keep the relationship too positive. The student will be fearful of reacting to the therapist teacher, of bringing in any kind of negativity because there will be a deep fear of losing the love and intimate connection that the Inner Child so desperately craves.

As we have pointed out, this is a very natural part of the consciousness process. If it is understood by the teacher, the student is helped to become aware of his or her vulnerability and is trained to recognize that the ultimate responsibility for one's Inner Child belongs to oneself. Once the seeker is able to begin to move in this direction, then we have a condition of awareness beginning to develop, and the person begins to be able to embrace both power and vulnerability.

As this process develops, the nature of the gratitude begins to go through a major shift. The seeker is still grateful for the help, love, good feeling, and everything else that was given to him or her. In addition, however, there is a development of personal power, a willingness to take risks in showing feelings and having reactions that might rock the boat. It is safer now to take such risks because the outer teacher is no longer the parent of the Inner Child. It is ourselves now with our own awareness who is parent to our own child.

Gratitude is an emotion that generally opens up the pores of love and compassion. In the healing arts, it is basic to the emotional bonding of the teacher/student interaction. Without awareness, it can lead to an excessive emphasis on positive feeling, with a resulting dependency and overemphasis on love and gratitude and compassion.

With awareness, these emotions can be fully experienced and appreciated without interfering with the ultimate empowerment process of the student, which should properly be our ultimate goal as teachers.

❤   ❤   ❤

Gratitude As a Way of Being

Dr. Sharron Stroud

__Dr. Sharron Stroud__, the International Woman of the Year in 1991-92, has been a Jungian theologian, inspirational speaker, counselor, and teacher for 25 years. She is also the founder of the Center for the Celebration of Life, a spiritual center that teaches, heals, empowers, and supports causes such as World Peace, abused women and children, and aids; and The Challenge Center, a treatment center where paraplegic and quadriplegic individuals rebuild their lives. She has also served as president of the United Clergy of Religious Science.

♥ ♥ ♥

I have discovered that gratitude is a way of being. When we become cognizant that everything in this life is a gift from the universe, and what we make of this thing called "life" is our gift back to the universe, our awareness is deepened. Gratitude is a tangible substance emanating from the person feeling this emotion. This substance permeates and pervades environments, clothing, and objects.

Gratitude as a "way of being" begins to manifest itself as the art and science of blessing. It makes sense when we realize that all life operates on a vibrational frequency of energy. The energy that we bring to life is the same energy that returns to us. This gets tricky when we don't receive the results in life that we want. However, each experience redeems itself through our willingness to get its message and accept the gift it offers in its wake. This creates the space for miracles.

When I was a child, we lived on a half-acre of walnut trees, and I had a "special" tree that I could climb up and be cradled by. The tree was such a special friend, and I was so grateful to have its companionship. The tree always listened to my every thought and allowed me to climb her limbs so I could have a "bird's-eye view" of the world around me. If I were hungry, she gave me her sweet meat, and I was satisfied. I could also make little boats from the walnut shells with a paper sail and a toothpick pole to hold it up with. Yes, the tree was my friend, and I was grateful.

When there was no external means of support in our family, my mother would hire migrant workers to shake the trees, and she and I would fill the gunny sacks full of the most beautiful walnuts on God's green earth. The sale of the walnuts always provided us with the most glorious Christmas. At the time all of this was going on, I did not have an appreciation for my mother's resourcefulness. Walnuts carry a dark skin around them that literally dyes one's hands black! It has to wear off gradually, so the kids at school would make fun of me, and the teachers would tell me to go and wash my dirty hands!

Years later, I would reflect on this experience and feel an overwhelming sense of gratitude, for it taught me to look at what is available in the immediate moment, to bless it, and watch its essence increase for my good! It also gave me a deep compassion for those who need our understanding and love in difficult situations—and, most importantly, to see the love that generates the activity before us.

The "attitude of gratitude" has served me well during my 20 years in the ministry. The art of blessing comes through in our willingness to let go and surrender to the Angel of the Presence who carries Beauty in Her wings—realizing that something is operating under the surface, and we must trust the process.

Being Authentic
Sets Us Free

Angela Passidomo Trafford

Angela Trafford *is the author of THE HEROIC PATH: ONE WOMAN'S JOURNEY FROM CANCER TO SELF-HEALING. When Angela was first given the "gift" of cancer, she saw that it was soon to become a pathway to the transformation in her life. After going through a series of chemotherapy and radiation treatments, she discovered Dr. Bernie Siegel's book LOVE, MEDICINE & MIRACLES and began to practice the visualization techniques outlined in it. As a result of her extraordinary healing experience (recounted in Dr. Siegel's book PEACE, LOVE & HEALING), Angela developed the gift of "seeing into people" to help* *them transform their own lives, their health, and their way of living. She currently teaches people how to live through the power of belief and love.*

"The quality of mercy is never strain'd; it falleth as a gentle rain from heaven...."

These words come to mind when I feel gratitude for the unconditional love in my heart—love that flows from the source of creation because I know I am forgiven.

Why do I need forgiveness? Why do I need to forgive? Because I am human.

As I practice forgiving myself and others, I feel the swell of gratitude moving within me, humbling me each moment in the proof of God's generosity. Gratitude moves my heart, bringing tears to my eyes. It is humbling to realize that I am loved.

This realization opens me up and allows me to grow. I feel a deep connection—communion with God and deep love for another human being. Someone has taken the risk to care about me, and for this miracle, I am grateful!

Gratitude links us with God and our fellow human beings. When I perceive a lack of gratitude in the world, I realize that in our woundedness, we have become isolated human beings, fearful of connection. We are rejecting the experience of intimacy that will truly engage us heart to heart in spiritual union with a fellow human being; we are rejecting our soulfulness.

In the early days of my healing work, I became despondent, perceiving a lack of gratitude in some of my clients who came to me for help.

I read the words of Albert Schweitzer in a sermon given at his mission in Africa. Quite simply stated, he said that if you feel a lack of gratitude, look within yourself and see if you are expressing gratitude.

I began living these words and found that my world changed. Being authentic is the only thing that truly works and sets us free.

Once, years ago, I was walking with a friend in a beautiful garden. I stopped, horrified to see a dragonfly quivering in the web of a large black spider. As I watched, the movements of the trapped dragonfly awakened the spider, who began to creep slowly toward its unfortunate prey. I could feel the plight of the dragonfly. It was fighting for its life!

Compassion drove me to reach quickly for a stick, and in an instant, I had freed the dragonfly, much to the dismay of the hungry spider. I brought my new friend to a nearby bench and carefully removed the sticky web from its feelers and legs. The sunlight glinted in pools of iridescence from its gossamer wings. I had always feared dragonflies; now I found this one fascinatingly beautiful.

The dragonfly perched on my finger, in no hurry to fly off. I found this amazing. After a long while, I wished it well and blew it away, as you would a ladybug.

It flew off and then returned, lighting on my shoulder, where it stayed most of the afternoon. You might think I'm silly, but I could swear it was thanking me!

Since then, I have had a close relationship with the dragonfly kingdom. In my secret heart, I imagine that I've rescued the king of the dragonflies and now, wherever I go, I am a welcome guest in their natural sanctuary, the earth. I don't know, but experiences such as these make me feel good inside.

A friend tells me he once rescued an owl, and it visited the tree by his bedroom window for years. I wish we humans could be as natural.

Gratitude: A Silent, Unspoken Prayer

Rama J. Vernon

Rama J. Vernon is the founder of the California Yoga Teachers Association, which is the founding organization and publisher of the YOGA JOURNAL. Rama's international work as president of the Center for International Dialogue (founded in 1984 to create a framework in which the citizens of the US and the USSR could overcome their differences through dialogue) and her vast background in yoga has led her to co-found the Institute for Conflict Resolution and Peace Studies. The Institute uses East-West psychology, spiritual principles, and Patanjali Yoga Sutras as the basis of inner/outer nonviolence training to create international teams of conflict-resolution specialists.

A great seer once said, "The angels hover over the earth looking for the rays of thanksgiving and gratitude that radiate from a selfless heart."

The word *gratitude* is defined by Webster as the quality of feeling or being grateful. (Great-full) or (thankful) means filled with greatness or grace. Gratitude is the giving of thanks, not one day a year, but every day, every minute, and with every breath. Its expression within our lives and with others blossoms into the realization that we are whole and complete within ourselves.

Gratitude has always been like a prayer, silent and unspoken for me. When sent forth from the center of our soul, it acts like a winged messenger transforming personal ambitions and petitions of needs and wants into a transcendent view of life's cycles and patterns.

When gratitude and thanksgiving become a way of life, all abundance—physical, spiritual, and material—co-exist simultaneously; our personal power mingles with the powers of the universe to heal the world as we heal ourselves. Gratitude carries us to the heights of the higher vibratory frequencies transforming cellular pockets of tension and dis-ease.

As we express gratitude with every breath, we become a symphony of compassion, love, and understanding, Borders of separation within dissolve into an awareness of our Oneness with All.

Even in life's darkest moments, we can open ourselves with reverence and great-fullness, knowing that crises give birth to new opportunities. With the joy of acceptance and thanksgiving, life's events flow like a steady, gentle stream of consciousness, transforming stumbling blocks into stepping stones.

Gratitude is our offering to a higher power, having faith that there is something greater than ourselves that is guiding, holding, and protecting us. The practice of gratitude is an offering that creates a field of resonance that unifies and empowers our vision of personal and global transformation.

How does one practice gratitude? You can practice gratitude each day with each word, each thought, and each gesture. Even though you may have lists of needs and wants, ask yourself what it is you have to be grateful for now. Look for things that trigger gratitude in your life, even if they may seem insignificant at first. Soon you will automatically begin to feel buoyant and joyful. Practice celebrating thanksgiving—not once a year, but every day. Make a gratitude list, and watch it grow. Focus on the abundance now existing in your life, rather than the lack.

Hold the vision of your life as being complete and whole. Affirm it. Realize it. Be it. There is nothing to reach for beyond yourself. You are the universe, contained in its own perfection. As Shakespeare once said, *"Assume the attitude, tho' you have it not, and it shall be yours."*

You can practice gratitude anytime or anywhere. To do this, simply become conscious of your breathing. As you breathe in, imagine the universal consciousness being pulled in from all directions simultaneously into the center of your Being. Hold your breath comfortably as you allow yourself to luxuriate in a sensation of fullness and completeness. As you breathe out, spread your inner fullness, joy, and abundance to all within your life and within the world.

A few other suggestions that I have found helpful over the years in cultivating a spirit of gratitude are:

♥ *See all people in the light of universal love while you work and walk beside them.*

♥ 285

♥ *Let your words heal rather than wound.*

♥ *Be the first to forgive and take the first step.*

♥ *Hold every person within your life with love and thanksgiving (especially those with whom there have been past or present difficulties).*

♥ *Be a spontaneous channel for the outpouring of unconditional love wherever you are, whomever you're with.*

♥ *Embody the peace you would like to see within the world.*

For me, gratitude is an attitude of mind and heart. It starts from within and flows through every part of my soul. It leaves no area of my being untouched. It encompasses all that I am and asks for the highest and best that I can envision and aspire toward. For me, gratitude is a state of being rather than doing. It is unending love for the Creator and all of life's creations.

Unconditional Gratitude

Doreen Virtue, Ph.D.

Doreen Virtue, Ph.D., is a fourth-generation metaphysician who maintains a counseling practice specializing in identifying and manifesting true purpose and desire. She is the bestselling author of LOSING YOUR POUNDS OF PAIN, CONSTANT CRAVING, and "I'D CHANGE MY LIFE IF I HAD MORE TIME"; and appears often on radio and television shows, including Oprah, Sally Jessy Raphael, Leeza, Montel Williams, and CNN. She is a contributing editor and advice columnist for COMPLETE WOMAN magazine, and a frequent contributor to WOMAN'S WORLD magazine.

*"Every situation, properly perceived, becomes
an opportunity to heal."*
— A Course in Miracles

It's easy enough to feel gratitude during the obvious moments, like when a friend goes out of her way to help you, or when you receive a gift especially suited to your liking. We readily ooze gratitude during spiritual moments: a powerful church service, an intense meditation session, or when a problem is miraculously resolved in the nick of time.

But what about those other moments—the ones not so obviously calling for gratitude? Is it possible to stay centered in appreciation when we really don't appreciate what's going on around us?

So often, our gratitude skips beats like a record with a gash across its center. When situations seem to warrant it, our hearts swell with appreciation. The other moments, though, we forget the eternal powers that are constantly wafting through our lives. We figure, "What's to be grateful for?"—that is, unless we are open and aware of the delicate and subtle lessons and miracles backdropped against everyday moments. Because, in truth, there is *always* something for which to be grateful.

God's awesome power is constantly at work, giving us exactly what we need in order to learn and grow. Universal law automatically and instantly gives us steady streams of opportunities to discover valuable truths about ourselves. We always attract the perfect lesson that suits our current blockages, desires, or questions. We don't need to do anything except notice these lessons as they come to us. If we don't recognize the opportunities inherent in these situations, we'll continually repeat them over and over again until we finally get it.

Gratitude is our way of saying to all situations, "Welcome! I've been expecting you! Thank you for being here to help me learn and grow." We are always stronger, wiser, and filled more with peaceful power when we face each of life's lessons with this sort of grace. Gratitude demonstrates to us and to the universe that we trust in Spirit's law of cause and effect. We fearlessly face each situation with the certain knowledge that it is merely an effect of our thoughts. No situation is a punishment or a reward. It is simply an effect.

Therefore, every situation in which we find ourselves is an opportunity to look in the mirror and see a perfect reflection of our thought patterns. All our situations—whether we'd label them negative or positive—are products of our thoughts. It is impossible, in this orderly universe, to randomly attract a situation not suited to your thoughts. If we don't care for the pattern of situations we are attracting, we can confront its source: our thought patterns. Spiritual growth comes from discovering thought patterns that don't suit you, and then deciding to replace them with healthier thoughts. It's a little like weeding a garden.

No matter what the form or physical appearance of situations in your life, see them as teachers lovingly sent to you for your highest and best good. These teachers are your guides to help you identify and break free of limiting and fear-based beliefs. Through these teachers, you learn to trust and lean on God's reliability and love. And the more you lean on God, the more you open the floodgates to your supply of harmony and abundance.

One of my counseling clients dramatically discovered the benefits of unconditional gratitude. Immediately before our telephone counseling session, I had been meditating, and so was very centered in Love. The first thing she told me was that her car had suddenly fallen into mechanical disrepair, and that she could not afford to pay the several hundreds of dollars required to fix the car.

Spontaneously, I declared, "Wonderful! God must have something great planned for you. Let's give thanks to Him."

My client, a woman of great faith, took a deep breath and hesitated for maybe a moment. Then the spirit of my request swept through her. She replied, "Okay, I want to have faith that this will work out for the best. But I have no idea how..."

"The *how* is up to God, not us," I counseled. "Let's just give thanks and know that all your needs have already been supplied." She and I joined in prayerful thanks to our Creator. We both knew that this situation was a doozy and that these types of situations always result in unforgettable demonstrations of Spirit's power.

We talked until she honestly felt at peace with the situation and was truly able to trust that her needs were already supplied. The basic principles of manifesting echo Jesus's words in the Bible: *"Whatsoever ye shall ask in prayer, believing, ye shall receive."* Successful manifestation depends upon three factors: affirming that your needs have already been met, believing that this is true, and being grateful for your supply. When my

client was able to peacefully hold these three factors in her thoughts, I asked her to then release
the situation to God. At that point, her manifestation of resolving her car situation was inevitable
because she had just demonstrated unconditional
gratitude.

I'm always grateful when a client attracts something akin to walking through a ring of fire. I
know that once a person faces a frightening situation while holding Spirit's hand, she'll never
again think she's alone in the Universe. She'll
know—from first-hand experience—that she can
always trust in God. Following the resolution of
these emotionally wrought situations, everyone
always ends up trusting themselves and God
more than they did previously.

My client called me soon after our session with
good news. "You were right, Dr. Virtue!" she
practically screamed into my car with enthusiasm. "Out of the blue, one of my co-workers
gave me her used luxury car for a bargain-

basement price, and she only wanted $100 as a down payment!"

Ever since my client's demonstration of putting her trust in God, she's never been the same. She now recognizes challenges as the opportunities for growth that they truly are. Her life has zoomed ahead at light speed because she no longer fears that she's alone or in danger. She now knows the truth that is true for all:

Gratitude gives us altitude above all
earthbound concerns and worries.
With unconditional gratitude, we are assured
of eternal abundance and growth.

Step to the
Infinite Self Within

Stuart Wilde

*Author and lecturer **Stuart Wilde** is one of the real characters of the self-help, human potential movement. His style is humorous, controversial, poignant, and transformational. He has written 11 books, including those that make up the very successful Taos Quintet, which are considered classics in their genre. They are: AFFIRMATIONS, THE FORCE, MIRACLES, THE QUICKENING, and THE TRICK TO MONEY IS HAVING SOME. Stuart's latest book is INFINITE SELF: 33 STEPS TO RECLAIMING YOUR INNER POWER. Stuart's books have been translated into 12 languages.*

♥   ♥   ♥

Our spiritual process through life is the journey from ego to spirit. Because the ego is usually insecure, it has many needs and impulses to gratify, and many fears it must assuage. The ego has to sustain its ideas and the precious image it has of itself. Attitudes become sacrosanct.

It is natural that the human personality, and the ego that dwells within that personality, would gradually, through self-confirmation, crown itself king or queen of all it surveys. Over time, orders and desires of that royal personage become edicts that cannot be challenged or broken. Keeping the king happy and giving the ol' slob what he wants become "Job One."

If a person is very bright or quite successful in human terms, it doesn't usually take him or her long to elevate oneself to the status of a demigod. Once the ego/personality has invested itself as a god, then extremes of self-importance flow from that. Orders are given, demands are made, and situations are manipulated. Softness, spirituality, and appreciation are repressed. Anyone defying the king and queen's edicts, or the image they hold of themselves, will feel the full wrath of a despotic regime.

Our modern society breeds despots. Compared to our ancestors, things are cozy and self-indulgent. All the ego will ever need is at its fingertips. We don't dig for food, chop trees, haul sewage— things are provided almost effortlessly. In these conditions, it is natural that humans would lose sight of gratitude, investing instead in accolades and importance; we become slaves to the effort of trying to keep the ego-king or queen happy.

And there you were, suddenly, a spiritual being in a diaper, born into a strange world of gratification and self-importance, indulgence and mayhem. One so young has no way of challenging the collective legislation of the ego. Soon you were trained to compete and strive and demand. You were taught the need to keep the ego happy at all costs.

History is the story of conflicting political egos and their struggle for importance and power. Your personal history tells of the same wars and struggles, treaties that were written, territories that were conquered, the struggles you went through sustaining the kingdom of *self*. In the turmoil of these self-centered laws, the sight of God is lost, and the reason and meaning of life are set aside. Spirituality, for most, is an underground resistance movement that scurries about in dark alleys when the ego sleeps.

So what of the quest for the holy grail, the sacred journey? To me it seems to be a journey of just under 12 inches, as we travel from the head to the heart, from thinking into feelings, from demands and gratification to appreciation and humility. The spiritual journey culminates in the death of the ego and the crowning of spirit.

As I mentioned in my book *Whispering Winds of Change,* the story of the crucifixion is a symbolic teaching that represents our spiritual journey. You see the ego/personality epitomized by the Nazarene, dying on the cross, racked with anguish. Mary Magdalene and the other women at the foot of the cross represent the *yin* softness of our infinite, spiritual self that can do nothing to save the ego. The women can only wait.

Once the Nazarene dies, he is placed in a tomb for three days. That is symbolic of silence, meditation, and prayer. It represents introspection, discipline, humility and gratitude—qualities you take on as you journey inward through the dark caverns of the inner self. During the introspection and healing, you prepare for the awesome presence of the Holy Spirit, the return of God in your life.

After the three-day period in the tomb, the Nazarene rises from death to ascend into heaven, at which point he assumes a new identity—he becomes *Christos,* the Divine Light—infused with the living spirit, immortal, returned once more to the presence of God.

Our journey is the same. On this holy journey, we heal ourselves, and we contribute to the overall healing of the planet, for nothing will be right until the ego is deposed.

Put away foolish things that cannot last. Embrace spirit with humility and gratitude, and step to the infinite self within. It seems to me a beautiful thing, that deep within us all, we each know how to make that sacred journey.

I feel truly thankful to live in this modern age, so cozy and fairly effortless. It is such a perfect time in history for making personal breakthroughs and spiritual transitions. Cool, utterly cool, in my view.

The Most Amazing Day

Margaret Olivia Wolfson

Margaret Olivia Wolfson is an internationally acclaimed storytelling artist and personal growth consultant. Her unique performances, presented with music, have delighted audiences at the Kennedy Center, the United Nations, the Sydney Opera House, the National Theater, and Princeton and Harvard Universities, to name just a few. She is the author of THE TURTLE TATTOO: TIMELESS TALES FOR FINDING AND FULFILLING YOUR DREAMS, and MARRIAGE OF THE RAIN GODDESS. Margaret lives in New York City.

♥ ♥ ♥

I thank you God for this most amazing
day: for the leaping greenly spirits of trees
and a blue true dream of sky; and for everything
which is natural which is infinite which is yes.
— e.e. cummings

Outside my window is a scene of breathtaking beauty. Tree-topped cliffs tower along the river, and each time the sun tumbles loose from the summer clouds, it splashes the leaves with light and glitters the river with gold.

Inside, more images nourish my eye. A Buddha, his eternal belly laugh masterfully captured by a Filipino woodcarver, stands on a cherrywood table—a cluster of quartz crystals twinkling at his feet. A grouping of photos—family, friends, and faraway places—rounds out the charm of this display.

Further contributing to this most amazing day is a feeling of contentment—arising from the fact that I am engaged in a cherished activity. I sit and write in a clean and peaceful apartment, a cup of apple blossom tea nearby, its steam swirling upward, sweetening the air. Taking all this in, I am overwhelmed with a soul-warming feeling that can best be described as gratitude.

It is also important for us to express gratitude—within reason—for all those things that challenge, sadden, anger, or frustrate us. As the poet Theodore Roethke writes, "In a dark time, the eye begins to see." As a storytelling artist, I have encountered many myths and tales that vivify this idea. Many of these stories teach us that serpents and toads—creatures often associated with the repugnant—are in fact the guardians of precious jewels and gold. Similarly, painful experiences are not meaningless. When we crack open pain's shell, we almost always discover spiritual pearls.

I once had a workshop participant whose story beautifully illustrates the power of gratitude. This woman, Marisol, bore the scars of inner-city life. Despite the fact that one parent was a hard and steady worker, the other was alcoholic and mostly absent. The abuse Marisol suffered at the hands of this parent, when combined with her childhood education in the dog-eat-dog mean streets of the city, eventually led to her downfall. Her soul collapsed, and she slid into the hellish underworld of drugs.

When Marisol turned 30, she became pregnant. She also learned she was HIV positive. Motivated by fear and imminent motherhood, she suddenly had one dream—to change her life. Toward this end, she began seeking help. Because she expressed profound gratitude to the administrators, counselors, facilitators, clergy, peers, and medical practitioners involved in her case, many went out of their way to assist her. Their support, when combined with her own formidable powers, worked a miracle.

As of this writing, Marisol is well on her way to a recovery from substance abuse, and in spite of the HIV, her health is good. The energy she once freely burned in the bowl of a crack pipe is now being used to create a future—however long or short it may be—for herself and her daughter—a sparkly-eyed, chubby-legged toddler of two.

Feeling and expressing gratitude for the good we have in our lives doesn't give us permission to passively accept the aspects of our lives that are not working. However, as we labor to spin the straw of lack into gold, we must focus on our wealth, not our poverty. And while we must consciously make an effort *not* to push away or avoid our problems, it is imperative that we simultaneously find things to praise. Complaining only focuses our mind's attention on what is missing, and what we mentally focus on gradually takes shape in the outer world.

One way we can develop our sense of gratitude is to pay closer attention to the beauty around us. Even seemingly small events such as quenching our thirst with a frosty glass of water, luxuriating beneath a quilt on a blustery morning, watching the breeze undo a dandelion puff, or listening to a chorus of crickets croaking and singing on a moon-gold night, are things that, if respectfully regarded, can summon up our gratitude.

Sadly, our lack of gratitude manifests itself in myriad ways, some of them not always obvious. For example, too many of us rush through life— ignoring its splendors as we plow through mind-boggling lists of activities. We pass through land-scapes exploding with color, but hardly notice. We wolf down our food, without even so much as a silent thank you to the living thing that gave its life for our nourishment. Others do kind or helpful things, and we minimize their efforts or express inadequate appreciation for the services performed. We fling beautiful books to the floor, taking their creamy, crisp, wisdom-packed pages for granted. Wrapped up in the demands of our personal lives, we too often ignore, or speak harshly to, the web of friends, family members, and colleagues who support us in our journey through life. The very source of existence, the sun, is all too often greeted with a curse, a grumble, and a groan; it is seen as a demanding intruder who orders us to throw off the covers of sleep and begin the activities of an unwanted day.

Many Native American traditions emphasize the importance of expressing gratitude, particularly to the earth. Like many, I am drawn to the solemn beauty of the Navajo Blessingway Chants. It is said that the power of these ceremonial songs is so great that they can bring the afflicted individual back into harmony with the world.

Not long ago, I saw a documentary that featured a Navajo singer reciting a version of the Beautyway Chant to an elderly woman. The chant, meant to quell the woman's anxiety, described the patient's connection to the spirit of the mountains, herbs, evergreens, morning mists, clouds, gathering waters, dew drops, and pollen. By helping this person feel kinship with the rich and wild beauty around her, the singer contributed to her healing.

In a similar way, the act of feeling and expressing gratitude *is* good and powerful medicine. When we feel connected to the richness surrounding us, we feel blessed. And although life and suffering are intertwined—paired together as rainbows and storm clouds, sunlight and shadow, sickness and health—gratitude, like faith, helps us understand that suffering is not the whole picture.

Gratitude Prayer

♥ ♥ ♥

by Louise L. Hay

Deep at the center of my being there is an infinite well of gratitude. I now allow this gratitude to fill my heart, my body, my mind, my consciousness, my very being. This gratitude radiates out from me in all directions, touching everything in my world, and returns to me as more to be grateful for. The more gratitude I feel, the more I am aware that the supply is endless. The use of gratitude makes me feel good; it is an expression of my inner joy. It is a warm fuzzy in my life.

I am grateful for myself and for my body. I am grateful for my ability to see and hear, feel and taste and touch. I am grateful for my home, and I take loving care of it. I am grateful for my family and friends, and I rejoice in their company. I am grateful for my work, and I give it my best at all times. I am grateful for my talents and abilities, and I continually express them in ways that are fulfilling. I am grateful for my income, and I know that I prosper wherever I turn. I am grateful for all my past experiences, for I know that they were part of my soul's growth. I am grateful for all of nature, and I am respectful for every living thing. I am grateful for today, and I am grateful for the tomorrows to come.

I am grateful for Life
now and forever more.

MY OWN THOUGHTS ON GRATITUDE...

❤   ❤   ❤

_____

_____

_____

_____

_____

_____

_____

_____

_____

_____

_____

_____

_____

_____

_____

GRATITUDE

GRATITUDE

♥ ♥ ♥

We hope you enjoyed this Hay House book.
If you would like to receive a free catalog
featuring additional Hay House books
and products, or if you would like
information about the Hay Foundation,
please write to:

Hay House, Inc.
P.O. Box 5100
Carlsbad, CA 92018-5100

or call:
(800) 654-5126

♥ ♥ ♥